Elevate

Jesus' Global Revolution For Women

By
Dr. Elena Garcia McKean

Elevate

JESUS' GLOBAL REVOLUTION
FOR WOMEN

First Edition, 2016, by
SoldOut Press
International
www.soldoutpressinternational.com
All rights reserved.

President: Carlos D. Mejía
Managing Editor: Héctor H. Gómez
Creative Consultant: José Otero
Designer: Catherine Niño
Photography: Mike Purdy Photography

ISBN: 978-958-59574-0-4

Printed in
Bogotá D. C., Colombia

Endorsements

ELEVATE is easily the best book on women's ministry that I have ever read. Weaving solid Biblical teaching and moving personal accounts, Dr. Elena Garcia McKean inspires us to deeply value and appreciate Jesus as a loving and caring, yet powerful and empowering Lord and Savior. You will see the dynamic women's ministry as Jesus designed and executed it through totally committed disciples, which included the women that were in His inner circle. It is beyond encouraging to have this written account, which articulates the conviction and the life of one of our modern day heroes in the faith. Thank you Elena for leading in the women's ministry as you do, and just like Jesus – full of "grace and truth!"

Lucy Mejia
Women's Ministry Leader in Mexico City, Mexico

What is the role of women in church today? How should they serve? What should they be allowed to do? Dr. Elena McKean in *ELEVATE* gives revolutionary insight into these very topics through an in-depth study of the women in Jesus' ministry. Through her solid exegesis and her personal life stories, she sheds insight on how important women were to Jesus in His ministry and she makes undeniable connections to the importance of the role of women in the church today.

Helen Sullivan
Women's Ministry Leader in Orlando, Florida

This heart-felt book empowers women to see and step into their pivotal role in God's church as teachers, advisers and examples of righteousness for other women. There is no better woman to learn this from than the co-founder of God's modern day movement – Dr. Elena McKean!

Patrique Smellie
Women's Ministry Leader in Lagos, Nigeria

"Women completed the leadership of God's people." Elena shares from the Scriptures, the purpose and the importance Jesus had for women in His personal ministry. In short, I love this book! It opened my eyes in a way no other book has to the personal way that Jesus calls us to **ELEVATE** to be more than what we ever thought we could be. For years, Elena has inspired me personally as a friend, as a wife, as a mother, as a disciple, as a leader and now as a gifted writer to value my role in God's Kingdom and to see the impact we can have as women.

Kerry Willis
Women's Ministry Leader in Sydney, Australia

I have had the privilege of knowing Dr. Elena McKean and her husband Kip for the past 13 years. Through the years of our friendship both Elena and Kip have literally spent thousands of hours patiently training my husband and me in Biblical leadership and church-building principles, as well as offering their heart-felt advice on marriage and parenting. I am so grateful that she is now sharing her heart and wisdom with all of you in this life-changing book. **ELEVATE** masterfully takes readers on an eye-opening journey through two of the most profound chapters for women in the New Testament Scriptures. Dr. McKean shares vulnerably about her life story as a woman in the ministry, and provides a compelling and Biblically sound argument that Jesus elevated and empowered women as "equal heirs" (Galatians 3:26-27) in the Kingdom of God. I pray this book will touch millions of women in this lost world to let Jesus elevate their lives to greater heights!

Michele Williamson
Women's Ministry Leader in London, England

This book is both moving and fascinating! It proves from Scripture how Jesus' transforming love truly "elevates" women! I have known "about" Elena since 1998, but I have personally known her since 2004 and she practices all that she preaches to women in this marvelous book.

Lynda Perdigon Moreno
Women's Ministry Leader in São Paulo, Brazil

ELEVATE is a revealing insight into the ministry of Jesus and His view of women and their indispensable role in the church. Women and men everywhere will be inspired and encouraged by Elena's story and God's plan to honor women and their invaluable contribution to Biblical ministry work.

Michael Kirchner
Chairman of the Board of Regents International College
of Christian Ministries in Los Angeles, California

Women's lives around the world are filled with fears from violence, peer pressure, false values, health issues and concerns about their families. In this incredible book, Elena primarily elevates Christ, who always knows how to fill me with inner strength and peace. Each chapter elevated my heart more and more to rejoice in God's mercy as it will always triumph over judgment! My husband and I are praying for this masterpiece to be translated into Russian as soon as possible!

Elena Sirotkina
Women's Ministry Leader in Moscow, Russia

ELEVATE by Dr. Elena McKean is a must read book for every woman of God! This remarkable book highlights the value Jesus placed on women as He "elevated" them in a time where women were viewed by most as dispensable property. I was personally inspired as I gained a deeper appreciation of my value to God, and therefore I feel more intensely than ever the call to fulfill God's purpose for my life! I am continually amazed at how powerfully God has used Elena in her personal ministry and cannot wait to see how many more will be impacted through her writings! I know that this book will inspire so many women in Asia and all around the world!

Joan Bartholomew
Women's Ministry Leader in Metro Manila, Philippines

Someone said this was a book for women! Well, let me tell you, this is a book for every Christian man too! I am so grateful for Elena and her amazing impact in my life and the life of my wife. Truly she is a woman whose life of humility and kindness, coupled with unbreakable doctrine has saved both herself and her hearers. A gentle word breaks a bone, and I am walking out of "this read" in a body cast! Thank you Elena for being a wonderful woman of God and mother in the faith to me. Thank you for all the time and effort that went into this treasure of the Kingdom!

Dr. Tim C. Kernan D. Min.
Lead Evangelist of the City of Angels International
Christian Church in Los Angeles, California

What words can I say about my mother in the faith Dr. Elena Garcia McKean? This incredible book is not written by an ordinary person, but an extraordinary woman who is filled with a great love for God and His people. In Chapter 7, Elena writes, "Anyone can change." I did not always believe that. After falling away from God, Elena's love and compassion for me and my family helped nurse my faith back to believe that I could once more change and be used by God. Her impact on so many women particularly my daughter Avrie – who loves her dearly – will forever be evidence of God's grace and sovereignty in our lives. I recommend this book to anyone who wants to see how God elevates women and wants their faith to grow. You see it in this powerful book, but even more powerfully in Elena's life. Thank you Dr. Elena Garcia McKean for your powerful testimony.

Cory Blackwell
Former NBA player and Lead Evangelist in Chicago, Illinois

Dedicated to "mi amor favorito," my amazing husband, Kip, who has lovingly challenged, heroically protected, and gently guided me to live for God with a passion by continually directing me to focus on Jesus and His global revolution. In addition, this labor of love is dedicated to our three remarkable children – Olivia, Sean and Eric – who have supported me, been so loyal, and taught me so much about God's mercy. Lastly, this book is dedicated to our three precious granddaughters – Alicia, Scarlett and Savannah – who have brought me more joy than words can express.

Contents

Acknowledgements

I am so grateful to my amazing Father in Heaven for this opportunity to write a spiritual book for women that has many of the principles that God graciously taught me through the years. As a young woman, I delighted in reading and even grew to enjoy public speaking about women's issues. However in all my years in school, I detested writing. Yet as Martin Luther stated, "If you want to change the world, pick up your pen and write."

The essence of this book comes from my dissertation for my Doctorate Degree from the International College of Christian Ministries. Therefore, I am deeply indebted to all who poured themselves out to found and build this glorious university. Thank you Tim Kernan, Chris Adams, Andrew Smellie, Michael Kirchner, Kyle Bartholomew, Helen Sullivan and my incredible husband Kip.

Additionally, I would be amiss if I did not thank those women who prayed with me and for me, as they helped to type, edit and support me during this adventure. So thank you Helen Sullivan (again), Sharon Kirchner, Jeanne McGee and my dear Rebecca Rico. Of special mention is Shay Sears who helped me grind through the initial three chapters.

Thank you as well to Mike Purdy for the beautiful cover photo. You have a wonderful gift. Thank you Hector Gomez for your vision to found the Berea Publishing House many years ago, and now creating under that umbrella my publishers — SoldOut Press International. I am greatly humbled that you have made *ELEVATE* your very first book to be published. And thanks to Carlos and Lucy Mejia during this whole process for your sage advice, godly guidance, detailed editing and most of all for your uplifting support that turned a scholarly dissertation into prayerfully a book that emulates our Savior's "common touch."

I would like to thank my dear parents for the godly convictions that they instilled in me through which my life has been blessed by God. I am extremely appreciative to Papá and Mamá who, in helping me to write a more accurate account of my heritage, shared with me on various occasions painful memories about our family's early days surrounding our leaving their beloved homeland of Cuba. For my parent's sake, I am thrilled that the Spanish version of *ELEVATE* (light bold and italic) will be published at the same time as the English one!

Lastly, I would like to thank my adoring (and adorable) husband Kip. He served as a sounding board for many of my thoughts and gave guidance on how to organize them into a smooth-flowing narrative. Thank you "Babe" most of all for our glorious partnership of marriage that began on December 11, 1976 – almost 40 years ago!

Elena Garcia McKean
July 1, 2016

Introduction

Luke's Gospel centers on Jesus' "Global Spiritual Revolution!" First announced by Jesus in Luke 4, "Global Spiritual Revolution" is the theme of His first sermon in His hometown of Nazareth. To begin His message that day, Jesus stood and read Isaiah 61:1-2, *"The Spirit of the Lord is on me, because He has anointed me to preach good news to the poor. He has sent me to proclaim freedom for the prisoners and recovery of sight for the blind, to release the oppressed, to proclaim the year of the Lord's favor."* (Luke 4:18-19) After reading this passage, Jesus sat down and began His lesson with the words, *"Today this Scripture is fulfilled in your hearing."* (Luke 4:21) Thus, He announced that He was indeed the prophesied Suffering Servant of Isaiah – the long awaited Messiah!

The immediate response to Jesus' lesson was that *"all spoke well of Him and were amazed at His gracious words."* (Luke 4:22) Realizing that His audience had "missed" the real significance of His message, Jesus reminds the people about the two great prophets Elijah and Elisha. Jesus explains, *"I assure you that there were many widows in Israel in Elijah's time, when the sky was shut for three and a half years and there was a severe famine throughout the land. Yet Elijah was not sent to any of them, but to a widow in Zarephath in the region of Sidon.*

And there were many in Israel with leprosy in the time of Elisha the prophet, yet not one of them was cleansed – only Namaan the Syrian." (Luke 4:25-27) Seemingly, without any other words spoken, all the people in the synagogue that day became furious, grabbed Jesus on the spot, and took Him up on a cliff to throw Him down intending to kill Him. Of course, it was not Jesus' time, so Jesus just walked through the crowd and went on to Capernaum.

His hometown was enraged because Jesus' vision was *"to preach good news, to proclaim freedom, to release the oppressed, and to proclaim the year of the Lord's favor"* not only for the Jews but also for the loathed Gentiles! At the very beginning of His ministry, Jesus is controversial because He preaches a revolutionary spiritual vision to change the world – Jews and Gentiles! Note as well that another dimension of this revolution is that Jesus preaches about Elijah aiding a Gentile "woman" and Elisha healing a Gentile "man." Once again graphically portraying that He came to start a Global Spiritual Revolution, He spoke not only of a world of Jews and Gentiles, but also of a world of men and women! Consequently, Jesus initiated the true Women's Liberation Movement!

Growing up in the 60's and 70's in the United States as a "Cuban immigrant" provided a constant challenge for me to know how to think about myself as a "woman." Thankfully, I had a very supportive father who treated my mother, my older sister and me with great respect. As a "Cuban family," we weekly attended a very traditional church that was part of our culture and I saw a noticeably limited number of women involved in leadership roles, though there were more women than men in attendance. It appeared to me that the women in the church were suppressed. By comparison, there were many more opportunities to use women's gifts in the "secular world" – in the medical, educational, business, legal, governmental and benevolent fields.

During my high school years, America's "Women's Lib Movement" was at its height, and I eagerly embraced it! I felt an inner turmoil and rebellion towards the form of "Christian religion" that I was raised with and saw around me. Although I had been raised religious, my true spiritual journey began when, at 17, I started studying the Bible seriously for myself. I thank God for my older sister Carmen challenging me to do so!

Having continued to study the Bible passionately for now forty-three more years, it has been encouraging and groundbreaking to see how much God values women! I am very grateful to keep learning and sharing the Biblical principles that help women to see God's equal and amazing love for us since they have previously been highly overlooked and largely untaught! My husband of almost 40 years, Kip, has always encouraged and supported my being intensely involved in ministry and spiritual leadership. We have shared numerous Bible studies and discussions on how to inspire and empower more women to use their gifts in God's church to change our hurting world!

One of the greatest joys of my life is serving on the Faculty of the International College of Christian Ministries (ICCM) as the Dean of Women and as a Professor. It is a tremendous honor to teach students especially in regards to women's issues. In 2014, the ICCM Bachelor's Program focused on the Gospel of Luke. For one of my classes, in which I taught the women separately, I was assigned Luke 7-8. As I studied and prayed over these two chapters, it dawned on me that an extraordinary number of women were interacting with Jesus in very impactful ways. I went to my husband Kip and shared with him this "discovery!"

We discussed at length the uniqueness of these passages of Scripture. Except for the Books of Ruth and Esther, nowhere in all Scripture is there found the concentration of verses that focus solely on women as in Luke 7:11 – 8:56. In the light of what commentators call the "Journey Section of Luke" where Jesus goes from Galilee to Jerusalem in Luke 9:51 to Luke 19:44, we decided to embrace these passages as the "Women's Elevation Section!"

Women have been so beaten down through the centuries, especially in the name of God. Jesus' spiritual revolution elevated the status of women from secondary afterthoughts to *"equal heirs"* in the Kingdom of God. (Galatians 3:26-27) Though every verse in the Women's Elevation Section is not solely about women, all of the lessons and principles in this section apply to men and women.

Therefore, as Jesus elevated women, the modern church is compelled to do the same to change our very lost world.

    This book is a compilation of these intriguing interactions that Jesus had with numerous women at all stages of life from Luke 7:11 to Luke 8:56. Also addressed are the Biblical principles in this remarkable passage of Scripture that desperately need to be taught in God's church. Prayerfully, the many personal examples from my life – both the faithful and the faltering – will allow the reader likewise to appreciate God's gracious mercy and powerful love for women! This "Global Spiritual Revolution" which elevated women to be equal heirs of Heaven with men began in the first century and now must be reintroduced and applied in the twenty-first century!

prophetess, Aaron's sister, [at 87 years old][1] took a tambourine in her hand, and all the women followed her, with tambourines and dancing! Miriam sang to them: 'Sing to the Lord, for He is highly exalted!'" (Exodus 15:20-21 NIV 1984) Men and women must love and respect one another as "God's complete image" to powerfully witness to our lost world and to lead His glorious people!

Although the Bible has been foremost in my life, two other books have profoundly influenced me and confirmed several spiritual concepts in regards to women that I have come to believe over my many years of studying the Bible. These insights about women are powerfully conveyed through *Lost Women Of The Bible* and *Half The Church: Recapturing God's Global Vision For Women* both written by Carolyn Custis James. James writes in her book *Half The Church,* "The Bible calls us to raise our eyes and our aspirations and strive to be like God. Our identity as God's image bearers casts in cement a fundamental equality, dignity and purpose among all human beings – truth that if embraced and acted on would make the world a better place."[2] This is only possible through what Jesus did for us (men and women); He sacrificed Himself for us to have our many sins forgiven. Not to be taken lightly, these sins destroy our gifts and usefulness in God's Kingdom.

We also receive power to overcome our sinful natures through God's gift of His Holy Spirit. In Acts 2:38-42 many came to believe in Jesus through Peter's powerful preaching on the day of Pentecost. (The traditional date for this epic event is 33AD, but many scholars now believe it occurred in 29AD.) Peter not only calls for faith in Jesus dying on the cross for mankind and God raising Him from the dead, but he adds, *"Repent and be baptized, every one of you, in the name of Jesus Christ for the forgiveness of your sins. And you will receive the gift of the Holy Spirit..."* Many women were in this crowd of thousands in Jerusalem and responded to this amazing promise from God!

Another powerful Scripture that I have held onto and taught for many years in regards to my relationship with God and my identity as a woman is Galatians 3:26-29, *"So in Christ Jesus you are all children of God through faith, for all*

of you who were baptized into Christ have clothed yourselves with Christ. There is neither Jew nor Gentile, neither slave nor free, nor is there male and female, for you are all one in Christ Jesus. If you belong to Christ, then you are Abraham's seed, and heirs according to the promise." This Scripture clearly shows that men and women have equal access to God our Father and are equal heirs of salvation!

In James' book *Lost Women Of The Bible*, the author clearly defines the calling of a woman to be a **"suitable helper"** from Genesis 2:18. The Hebrew word for helper is **"ezer"** which is "used most often (16 of the 21 occurrences) in the Old Testament to refer to God as Israel's helper in times of trouble."[3] "Further research indicates that **'ezer'** is a powerful Hebrew military word… An **'ezer'** is a warrior."[4] For many years, I have felt called by God through the Bible, through my husband's awesome encouragement, and through discipling from other spiritual women to be a "strong warrior helper" not just in my marriage, but also for the rescuing of the souls of men and women on our crazy and fallen planet. At times, it has been an intense battle to rise above criticism and the traditional suppression of women through the "man-made ideas" of the church. After much prayer and constantly searching the Scriptures, I have embraced this inspiring calling from God because of the ultimate goal to help my husband as well as many others get to Heaven.

I must confess I did not grasp my calling from God when I was first married to a very loving, driven, dynamic and captivating young preacher of the Gospel. Thanks to the generosity of our parents, we had a beautiful wedding on December 11, 1976 where we joyfully and seriously took our marriage vows before our families and many friends "for better or for worse" to honor God and each other "till death do us part!" Our previous three-year dating relationship was pure and very helpful to my spiritual growth as Kip took care of me spiritually and emotionally.

Kip was a Chemistry Major two years ahead of me in college, so I deeply appreciated his help with one of my least favorite pre-requisite classes for

Occupational Therapy (OT) – Chemistry, since I was struggling. I was encouraged when I received an "A" in this class since it helped me accomplish my desire to be accepted into the Occupational Therapy Program at the University of Florida. We also had many fun dates going to the Gator football games, sharing meals, hiking and playing sports of all sorts, yes even tennis, but it was especially encouraging when we talked about our spiritual lives. We had great practical and Biblical guidance for our relationship through the "Christian family" in our church. Kip felt called to go into the full-time ministry after his younger brother was diagnosed with cancer (Hodgkin's Lymphoma) at the end of Kip's sophomore year. I admired his heart to serve God not thinking that my life would also be affected when we began "dating steady."

Kip was a leader of two campus weekly Bible Study groups and a teen Bible study group while simultaneously going to school full-time and serving as an officer in his Sigma Chi Fraternity. He also worked part-time as a janitor for our new larger church building. Since he no longer desired to be a medical doctor, he later changed his major to Speech Communications (after taking 36 hours in Chemistry) and was awarded upon graduation the highest academic award – Phi Beta Kappa! He was also training for the ministry with our two ministers through church planning sessions and running many of our college ministry events. He was very effective and zealous about the ministry. Kip was and is my favorite preacher!

I deeply respected his heart to serve in the full-time ministry, but my heart was to serve God through a medical career. I saw other strong women in our church with their own separate careers while their husbands served and were supported in the full-time ministry by the church. In that day, women serving in the full-time ministry were uncommon. During my junior year of college, Kip went off to his first "ministry position" in Philadelphia, Pennsylvania. I had just been accepted into the Occupational Therapy Program so we had a long-distance dating relationship. In actuality this deepened our communication through letters, a weekly Saturday night phone date, a few short trips he made to see me back in

Gainesville, and one trip where I traveled to see Kip's ministry in Philadelphia and stayed with a very kind leadership family (an elder and his wife) in the church for a weekend. It was very exciting to see how God was using Kip profoundly to help college students, but again I had no desire to serve in the full-time ministry because the women's role of leadership was very limited at that time. After our beautiful wedding, we had a super awesome honeymoon! I then moved to join Kip as his wife in the small university town of Charleston, Illinois where Kip served as the Campus Minister for the Heritage Chapel Church of Christ.

Charleston was a city of only 18,000 people centered around Eastern Illinois University – a campus of 9,300 students. The next closest city was Mattoon, 12 miles away with a population of 20,000. Moving from Florida during the middle of a cold Midwest winter was rough. God blessed me to secure two different Occupational Therapy internships of three months each about an hour's drive away – when the snow was well plowed off the roads!

Needless to say, it was total culture shock for me to be living in such a frigid place and as a "preacher's wife." I was leading three Bible Study groups for the college women in their dorms on different weeknights after long, intense, but rewarding days at my OT internship with stroke and brain disabled patients. In addition, every week I was attending mid-week Bible class for all of our church members and then a Friday night college devotional plus two services on Sunday. I was also trying to learn how to be a new wife in taking care of Kip and our home while hosting meals on the weekends for college students, as well as discipling four college women with weekly two-hour spiritual mentoring sessions.

After just two months of giving my best efforts and "living through" a blizzard where I was snowed in at work at the hospital, I started desperately missing "warm Florida" and all my closer church friends and my physical family. I did not know how to communicate all my feelings with Kip and I was extra emotional being on birth control pills. I was not a very strong or happy Christian at this point. My personal times with God were squeezed out by "burning the candle at both ends." I also did not see the older adults in the church as people I could talk with, because I was the "young preacher's wife." My life was now a "fish-bowl" where I received criticism from some of the older women in the church for wearing make-up, dressing too flashy since my wardrobe was more Florida style and college-aged, etc. Even the main minister who was very kind towards us did not always agree with what we were doing, and his wife seemed depressed and overwhelmed with her role as a preacher's wife and a mother of three little children. Sadly, I really enjoyed my OT internship more than being a preacher's wife. I cried out to God a lot and finally called the Gainesville minister's wife, Ann, who I admired and trusted in my "home church" (the Crossroads Church of Christ) to tell her how very sad and lonely I was. She was very compassionate and listened. Thank God, she and her husband came to Charleston a couple weeks later to speak at our first Midwest Evangelism Seminar that my husband had organized.

God taught us so much through this conference and especially through our face-to-face time with Ann, who served as a "Woman's Counselor" for the Crossroads Church. Kip was very humble in taking her advice on our overly zealous schedule, on how to better take care of me, and on how to listen more as a new husband. She helped me to see that my heart had become bitter and ungrateful for Kip in my sinful response to being hurt by withdrawing my heart and not communicating. Kip and I both saw God taking care of us. We realized that we needed a more mature and trustworthy Christian married couple in our lives to continue our spiritual growth in our marriage. We later began calling this – "marriage discipling." We also saw how critical it was to stay close to God through our own daily personal times with Him.

When Kip arrived in Charleston in the Fall of 1976 (I arrived four months later), he had only seven campus students. That said, in just three years God super blessed our college ministry at Eastern Illinois University with three hundred college men and women coming to faith and being baptized into Christ! After completing my internships, extra course work, and passing my Occupational Therapist Registered Board Exams, I continued working as an OT for a local hospital for twenty to thirty hours a week so I could still help with the women in our campus ministry, whom I had grown to love deeply.

This was also a time where God showed me the value of "Women's Days." Our little Midwestern church annually hosted a "Women's Day," inviting women from our community and surrounding Churches of Christ to come hear a lesson about being godly women. Following the lesson, they would do arts and crafts, and then have a delicious luncheon hosted by our "older women" who were incredible cooks! In my second year in Charleston, I was asked to organize the Women's Day and be the keynote speaker. We had some musical performances as well as a skit that related to both college and older women alike. Kip helped me with my lesson and how to deliver it powerfully, since I was not experienced in preaching. My lesson's theme was about Jesus and how much God loves and values us as women. Then we had a marvelous luncheon with fellowship to encourage and help one another. There were many tears, much laughter, hugs and deep spiritual discussions. This special time moved many of our guests to study the Bible with us and find spiritual healing! God was teaching me how as sisters when we worked together in using our many talents, we will have a great spiritual impact to help other women!

These two important ministry tools of "marriage discipling" and "Women's Days" were developed further when we moved to Boston to serve there in the ministry. In 1979, Kip asked me to help him more with the women and serve in the full-time ministry since Boston had so many colleges and a much larger population. I had to pray through mixed feelings of sacrificing my career and not being paid to serve in the ministry since married ministry women were not paid at that time. We were super blessed to have an older married couple – Bob and Pat Gempel – guide and strengthen our marriage through marriage discipling. They humbly allowed us to train them in leading Bible discussion groups, basic Christian counseling, and organizing ministry events. We committed to be totally unified as families for the sake of building up the church even though we had different marriage dynamics and perspectives. There was mutual respect and great affection between us! Kip and I are eternally grateful for this powerful couple that God put in our lives. Those earlier feelings of loneliness as a "preacher's wife" dissipated as my personal calling from God became clear and very fulfilling.

Lastly, another fascinating aspect of Luke 7:11-12, is the account of Jesus accompanied by a large crowd while entering into Nain, which all of the sudden comes face-to-face with another large crowd going out of this town mourning with this grief-stricken widow whose son had just died. The son was laying on a wooden plank, "a bier" not in a coffin, and most likely not covered with a cloth, as the Scriptures do not mention a covering. In the midst of these two crowds, Jesus displays His compassion for this one woman, not allowing himself to get caught up or lost in the bedlam of these two converging groups. Jesus was not thinking of himself, but rather how He could provide hope for a desperate woman in a seemingly very hopeless situation. This is the Jesus that came to "my rescue" in Charleston and in the years to come!

1.   Psikta Rabbati 43:27 Miriam is said to be seven years old when Moses was born.
2.   Carolyn Custis James, Half The Church, (Grand Rapids, Michigan: Zondervan, 2011), Page 55
3.   Carolyn Custis James, Lost Women Of The Bible, (Grand Rapids, Michigan: Zondervan, 2005), Page 35
4.   Ibid., Page 36

CHAPTER

2

Filled With Awe

Luke 7:14-17 – *Then He went up and touched the bier they were carrying him on and the bearers stood still. He said, **"Young man, I say to you get up!"** The dead man sat up and began to talk, and Jesus gave him back to his mother. They were all filled with awe and praised God. "A great prophet has appeared among us," they said. "God has come to help His people." This news about Jesus spread throughout Judea and the surrounding country.*

This is the priceless scene of Jesus' raising the widow's only son from the dead by commanding, **"Young man, I say to you get up!"** The situation is so amazing, amusing and incredible because the dead young man immediately sat up and began to talk! I wish we knew what he was talking about! As well, what an incredible sight of the shocked and happy mother once Jesus gave her son back to her! Here Jesus was called a **"great prophet"** because the Old Testament records only two prophets miraculously raising the dead. The first is Elijah in 1 Kings 17:17-24 who raises to life the son of the widow of Zarephath. The second is Elisha in 2 Kings 4:27-37 who raises to life the only son of the married Shunammite woman. (Interestingly, both of these women were Gentiles!) As one can easily imagine, the people who witnessed Jesus raising a dead young man to life were *"filled with awe"* and saw that God was with Jesus *"to help His people."* This magnificent news *"spread throughout Judea and the surrounding [areas of the] country."*

Escaping from Cuba in April 1959 with my father (Papá), my mother (Mamá), my seven-year-old brother Nick, my six-year-old sister Carmen, my eight-month-old baby brother Jorge, and myself (almost four years old) was an incredible life-changer for our entire family! We left because of Fidel Castro's communist revolution. Many Cubans at that time thought that Castro's new regime would be much better than the corrupt regime of the dictator Fulgencio Batista. However, Papá had attended Colegio de Belén – a prestigious all-boys Jesuit high school – with Fidel Castro. Being in the same class of about 35 young men for several years, Papá saw Fidel's "Marxist leanings" grow. According to Papá, Castro was not a man of integrity nor a very spiritual or family-oriented person, although he was very bright, charismatic and athletic. They graduated from high school together in 1945. I remember a few "Castro stories" that my parents shared with us, but they did not like to talk about these events, because it was such a painful and difficult experience.

In 1959, a month after the Castro takeover, 2,500 – 3,000 men were executed by gunfire as enemies of the revolution. Our home was to be taken by the Castro regime and no one would be allowed to own private property because all property would belong to the communist government. After Castro's bloody military takeover, my parents planned in one month to leave Havana and go to Key West on a ferry with our car and a few suitcases of clothing. They left everything else behind, including their parents and siblings. Castro even closed Papá's expansive and beautiful Colegio de Belén and turned it into army barracks. This too was another very painful occasion given that my parents were married in the gorgeous chapel on the Colegio de Belén campus.

Papá was a civil engineer with his own small consulting business in Cuba and he had done some work for an engineering consulting firm from Gainesville, Florida in Havana just a few years before. Therefore, he contacted this company, Black & Associates, for a job in Gainesville. They agreed to hire Papá and therefore he was able to get a work visa to leave Cuba with our family. He also asked the company if he could pursue his Master's of Science in Engineering specializing in water resources while working full-time to support our family. They were very supportive and the day after we arrived in Gainesville, Papá started working!

However, I felt like a "foreigner" (and indeed I was), because I only spoke Spanish, the native language of Cuba. Yet, my courageous Mamá knew that we all had to learn English very quickly to make our lives work. I remember crying on my first day of nursery school because I did not understand the other children. One young blonde, blue-eyed child gently grabbed my hand and took me to play on the monkey bars. In nursey school we became best friends and this relationship extended all through high school. Even to this day Cynthia and I keep in touch!

My Cuban family was one of the first Latin families in the small university town of Gainesville and so I was an "outsider." Gainesville was a very segregated community in the early 60's, but God was watching out for us through the house that my parents selected. Our house was directly across the street from the University of Florida Tennis Facility with numerous courts. (Tennis would later become my passion!)

Thankfully, we had kind and fun neighbors who helped to "Americanize" us. We celebrated Thanksgiving together in their home for the first time in 1959 and then in our home the following year. We alternated homes each year celebrating Thanksgiving through my high school years. I am deeply grateful for my parents who worked so hard to take care of us with very strict standards of behavior. We were required to speak Spanish in our home and we went to church every Sunday. We took Catholic Catechism Doctrine (CCD) Classes each week during the school year. My dad taught CCD Classes for a while and I remember my parents hosting

Spanish "Rosary Prayer" Meetings in our home with new "Latin families" moving into Gainesville! These Spanish gatherings were very uncomfortable for me, but I knew they were important times for my parents. This was their generous way of giving support to these incoming families. Along the way, they built many wonderful, life-long friendships.

These families were from many different Spanish-speaking countries, not just Cuba. Doctors, lawyers, engineers, educators and business professionals who were trying to re-build their lives in America came together to maintain some of their Spanish culture. As children, we were asked to play quietly in our rooms or else there would be consequences. So, naturally, I did not enjoy these events and could not relate to what was going on. My siblings and I wanted to be "Americans" and liked being with our American English-speaking friends much more!

Through much hard work and sacrifice, Papá completed his Master's Degree and went on to receive his Doctorate specializing in Environmental Hydraulics Engineering. Our lives were very blessed in material ways and my parents made numerous efforts to keep our family close. We ate dinners together most nights, went to church together almost every Sunday, and enjoyed great family vacations every summer to a beautiful beach spot or road trips to different parts of America where Papá participated in engineering conferences. My parents had achieved the "American dream" of owning their own home and car. Yet, I still felt like something was missing.

I had many insecurities about how I looked with my black hair, dark eyes and olive colored skin. Since I played tennis most days in the Florida sun, I developed a really dark tan which added to my insecurities! Now as a parent, I am grateful for how much my parents tried to talk with my sister and me about modesty issues. They taught us that how we dressed reflected our values. Our manners were also addressed. Mamá would take my sister and me shopping and guided us in our clothing selections to help us understand how much these items cost and to train us in dressing modestly.

During high school, my sister and I finally wore Mamá down to allow us to buy two-piece bathing suits, mini-skirts and bell-bottom jeans! In retrospect, I was becoming a "pseudo-hippy" conforming to the times and the more liberal culture of the university town we lived in. There were strong anti-Vietnam War feelings at the University of Florida and some of these more violent protests we could hear from our home. This was very disturbing to my parents because of all they went through with the Cuban Revolution. It was an eerie and rebellious time towards "the establishment" of the United States government, and in fact, all authority. I quietly drank deeply of this intoxicating message of rebellion.

Recently, Papá and Mamá celebrated their 65th Anniversary as their wedding day was on June 24, 1951 in Havana, Cuba at the gorgeous Colegio de Belén Chapel. They have been guiding lights to me throughout my life.

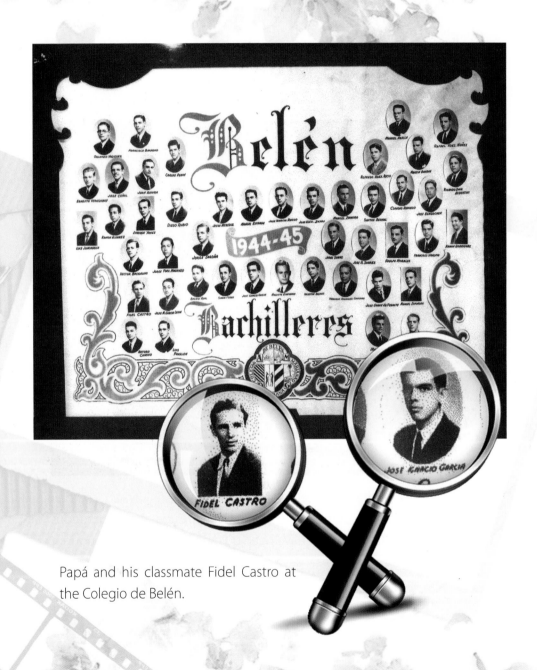

Papá and his classmate Fidel Castro at the Colegio de Belén.

"Mi Familia" a few months after arriving from Cuba to our new home in Gainesville, Florida. I am sitting on the floor between Papá and Mamá. My brother Nick is eight, Carmen is six, I am four, and Jorge is one year old. Peter was born eight years later.

"Mi Familia" is complete with the birth of my little brother Peter.

Even in my younger years, my "big" sister Carmen was always looking out for me.

The Donigans (center) were the kind neighbors who "Americanized" us. One of the most enjoyable times with our two families was celebrating Thanksgiving every year. I am on the far left envisioning eating the yummy turkey.

Our Noche Buena (Christmas Eve) celebration in 1967. (I am in the middle.)

Almost every Noche Buena we celebrated with my Tío Francisco and Tía Margarita (center, back row). I am seated on the left side of the couch next to my first cousin Javier — who became an accomplished neurosurgeon like his father — and my other first cousin Maruchi, who is truly a sister to me, is on the far right.

The next year in 1969, we again celebrated Noche Buena with my Tíos but in their home. I am sitting between Maruchi and Peter.

My sophomore class picture in 1970.

My junior class picture in 1971, shows my transition to becoming a "pseudo-hippy."

This is my PK Yonge High School Tennis Team, where I played number one singles both my junior and senior years. (I am standing in the center of the back row.) My coach "Miss D" (in the blue skirt) was a tremendous inspiration in my life.

PKY Gals In State

OCALA (Special-to-the-Sun) — Refusing to be denied, P.K. Yonge's proud girls tennis team trimmed Orlando Evans, 4-3, here Monday in a playoff for sole possession of second place and a berth in the state tournament later this week.

"The girls were under a great deal of pressure," PKY coach Babs Dalshiemer smiled afterwards, "but they wouldn't wilt. They wanted so much to do well, and they did."

Elena Garcia (No. 1), Lee Henderson (No. 3) and Meg Gallant (No. 4) in singles and Misses Henderson and Gallant, only a sophomore, in No. 2 doubles were PKY winners, but even the PKY losers were interesting in that Janice Fellars (No. 5) forced her foe Kathy Huber to two extended sets; Celia Martin (No. 2) lost

ELENA GARCIA
. . . Singles Winner

for only the second time in district competition all spring (and that to the same opponent): Evans sophomore star Nancy Cop-

pola; and the Garcia, Martin No. 1 doubles team fell to the best duo in the district: Coppola and Kathy Stillwell.

Monday's match, played in cloudy, cool weather here on a neutral court was especially sweet for the PKY gals in that it broke a three-game habit of finishing third.

Next on the agenda for "Dalshiemer's Dollies" is Wednesday's drawing for seedings for the three-day 50th annual state tourney beginning Thursday in Gainesville with the likes of the Evert sisters, Chris Jeanne of Fort Lauderdale's St. Thomas Aquinas High.

SINGLES — Elaine Garcia (PKY) def. Stillwell (E), 7-6, 6-3; N. Coppola (E) def. Celia Martin (PKY), 6-3, 6-4; Lee Henderson (PKY) def. Ford (E), 6-2, 6-2; Meg Gallant (PKY) def. A. Coppola (E), 6-0, 6-3; Buber (E) def. Janice Fellars (PKY), 7-6, 7-6.

DOUBLES — Stillwell, N. Coppola (E) def Garcia, Martin (PKY), 60, 6-4; Henderson, Gallant (PKY) def. A. Coppola, Huber (E), 6-3, 6-1.

This is the newspaper article in the Gainesville Sun that announced that the Women's Tennis Team of PK Young made it to State my junior year. Of note, Chris Evert of St. Thomas Aquinas High won the entire Florida Singles Championship.

My senior picture at 17 years old – the
age that I was baptized.

Carmen and I at the 1973 Florida Evangelism
Seminar just a few days after I was baptized.

Noche Buena in 1973 was celebrated with my Tíos and cousins.
(I am in the back row standing in between Mamá and Tío
Francisco.)

Kip and I when we first started "dating steady" in 1974.

Kip in 1975 – his first year of full-time ministry in Philadelphia.

ELENA GARCIA-BENGOCHEA

Garcia-Bengochea-McKean

Dr. and Mrs. Jose Ignacio Garcia-Bengochea, Gainesville, announce the engagement of their daughter, Elena, to Thomas Wayne McKean II, son of Capt. and Mrs. T. W. McKean, Moraga, Calif.

The wedding is planned for Dec. 11.

My wonderful engagement announcement in the *Gainesville Sun*.

Participating in my bridesmaids dinner party was my dear cousin Maruchi (left) and my beloved maid of honor Carmen.

Excitingly, on December 11, 1976, Kip and I were married at the Crossroads Church of Christ where about 800 gathered. Papá and Mamá are beside me and Kip's parents are next to him.

All dressed up to leave for our honeymoon in the Bahamas.

Graduate Schools of
THEOLOGY
PSYCHOLOGY
WORLD MISSION

Fuller Theological Seminary

School of World Mission

August 3, 1988

Rev. Kip McKean
Boston Church of Christ
P.O. Box 313
Boston, MA 02117

Dear Kip:

I want to thank you for your warm welcome during my visit to
Boston Church of Christ. I had known quite a bit about it previously,
but nothing can match actually seeing and hearing and feeling the mighty
work of the Spirit of God in your midst.

Thank you also for your letter and for sending the historic June 26
issue of your newsletter.

Kip, I want you to know that I am deeply impressed by what God is doing
through you and the churches you lead. This is one of the great works of
the Father in the transition to the 21st century.

I am well aware of the criticism which you have received, and (to use
a mild term) I am deeply distressed. Even since I have been telling others
of my recent visit, I have taken some flack. You obviously don't need my
support, but I want you to know that it is available to you for the asking.

Let's keep in touch!

Warmly,

C. Peter Wagner
Professor of Church Growth

CPW:pm

P.S.   Shadrach, Meshach and Abed-Nego would feel quite comfortable in the
Boston Garden! If they were here, they'd join your church.

Pasadena, California 91182 • Telephone: (818)584-5200/*Cable:* FULLSEM

As God began to give Kip's and my ministry a global impact we became more
and more controversial. However, we were greatly encouraged by C. Peter
Wagner's letter, as he was the professor of church growth at the prestigious
Fuller Theological Seminary.

Eric and Sean having a little summer fun in Thailand during our planting of the Bangkok Church in 1989… And yes, it is a real python.

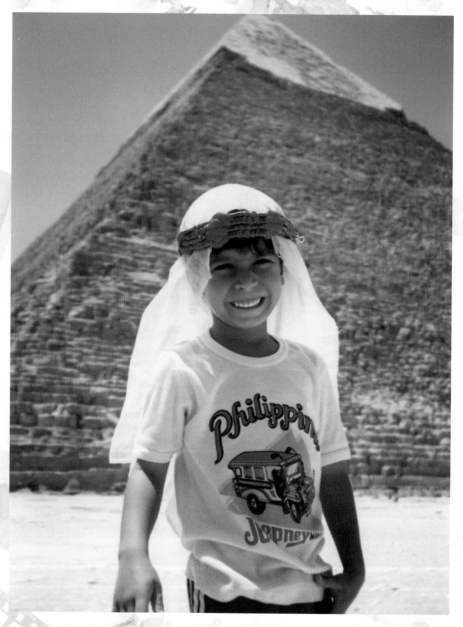

Eric enjoying the Egyptian culture at the base of the Great Pyramid of Giza in the summer of 1989.

Eric, Olivia and Sean in our backyard in Lexington, Massachusetts in December 1989.

In 1990, we visited in Tokyo Kip's and my spiritual grandparents — George and Irene Gurganus.

Eric, Sean and Olivia enjoying LA shortly after we moved there in 1990.

While visiting my parents in Gainesville, Florida, I took our three children to see the house where I grew up.

At 37 years old, my first head shots were taken
for my talent agency — Gilla Roos.

Olivia joins me for a mother/daughter
modeling shoot.

Our 1994 family picture was taken on Manhattan Beach.

In 1995, God allowed Kip as Chairman of the Board of HOPE*worldwide* to meet with President Nelson Mandela in Pretoria, South Africa to present him with the HOPE Unity Award and to invite him to church!

Bob and Pat Gempel walking with us in the Garden of Gethsemane just outside of Jerusalem in 1996.

Tony and Therese Untalan (left) as well as Nick and Denise Bordieri have been loyal partners in the Gospel from our first days in Portland in 2003 to these days in Los Angeles.

Matt and Helen Sullivan, dear friends, moved to Portland after the First Portland Jubilee in 2004. Later, they planted the Phoenix, Arizona; the Santiago de Chile; and the Orlando, Florida Churches.

The courageous and kindhearted missionaries, Raul and Lynda Moreno, visited us in Portland for the first time in 2005.

Santeri and Olivia's beautiful wedding in Helsinki, Finland in 2006. Both sets of grandparents honored us by their presence.

Eric served as the Captain of the Stanford Tennis Team during his senior year.

In the fall of 2006, Kyle and Joan Bartholomew's courageous stand in Hilo, Hawaii was the spark that God used to initiate His new SoldOut Movement.

Kip performed incredible wedding ceremonies for all three of our children. In June 2012, Sean & Alex's wedding was a beautiful outdoor occasion!

In the summer of 2012, mis queridos Papá y Mamá graciously celebrate my 57th Birthday!

In December 2012, Eric & Tiffany were married. At their wedding reception, they surprised us all with their first dance by dancing the tango to perfection!

Admiral Tom and Kim McKean — Kip's parents and my precious in laws — celebrating both of their 85th Birthdays at the end of 2013!

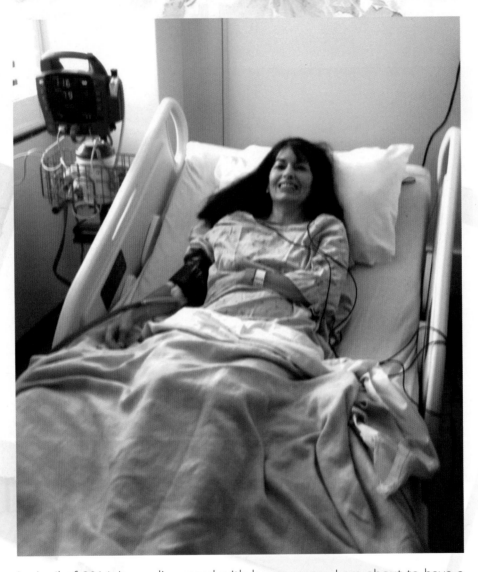

In April of 2014, I was diagnosed with bone cancer. I am about to have a bone marrow biopsy… Not fun!

Since our early Portland days, Tesoni Untalan and Coleen (Untalan) Challinor have been like daughters to Kip and me!

Announcing ZION'S DREAMERS – the 2014 GLC – are Tyler and Shay Sears with Rebecca Rico and me!

Amazingly, my 2015 Global Leadership Conference lesson was LiveStreamed into 69 countries!

Our dear daughter in the faith Rebecca Rico was the Valedictorian of the ICCM Class of 2015 at the Commencement Ceremony where I received my Doctorate Degree!

After the Sunday Service and the ICCM Commencement of the 2015 Global Leadership Conference, Kip hosted a great party and had a gluten-free specialty cake made to celebrate receiving my Doctorate Degree and turning 60 years old!

As MERCY Ambassadors, Joan Bartholomew, Kip and I served the underprivileged children in Metro Manila in 2015!

The gallant couple that God raised up to take the leadership of the City of Angels Church was Tim and Lianne Kernan, pictured with their adorable sons — Junior and David!

Michael, a former Vice President at General Mills, and Sharon Kirchner have been loyal partners in the Gospel since 2007 and tirelessly serve in the SoldOut Movement as the World Sector Leader Couple for Administration and Law!

Andrew and Patrique Smellie, a trusted son and daughter in the faith, inspired all of the SoldOut Movement by planting the dynamic Lagos (Nigeria) International Christian Church!

Carlos and Lucy Mejía, the closest of friends, have been indispensable in building the SoldOut Movement as well as helping me to publish this book! Their sons, Carlitos and Andrew, are grandsons to Kip and me!

One of our closest friends — Cory Blackwell, a former NBA player — and his daughter Avrie celebrating that she was Valedictorian of her High School!

Cynthia was my best friend from nursery school through high school, and we still have a heart connection!

My dear 18 year old granddaughter – Alicia! Sean and Alex, her parents and Abuelo Kip and I are very proud of her academic and dancing accomplishments. As well, Alicia was the Captain of her High School Soccer Team!

Sweet Scarlett – now three years old, is the first daughter of Santeri and Olivia. Already she is beginning to read!

Abuela tenderly held her third precious granddaughter, Savannah, at one day old. She looked so much like her mother Olivia when she was born.

Kip and I after praying on Diamond Head Mountain in Hawaii for the evangelization of the nations in this generation!

CHAPTER
3

The Purpose of God

Luke 7:18-30 – *John's disciples told him about all these things. Calling two of them, he sent them to the Lord to ask, "Are you the one who is to come, or should we expect someone else?" When the men came to Jesus, they said, "John the Baptist sent us to you to ask, 'Are you the one who is to come, or should we expect someone else?'"*

At that very time Jesus cured many who had diseases, sicknesses and evil spirits, and gave sight to many who were blind. So He replied to the messengers, **"Go back and report to John what you have seen and heard: The blind receive sight, the lame walk, those who have leprosy are cleansed, the deaf hear, the dead are raised and the good news is proclaimed to the poor. Blessed is anyone who does not stumble on account of me."**

*After John's messengers left, Jesus began to speak to the crowd about John: **"What did you go out to the wilderness to see? A reed swayed by the wind? If not, what did you go out to see? A man dressed in fine clothes? No, those who wear expensive clothes and indulge in luxury are in palaces. But what did you go out to see? A prophet? Yes, I tell you, and more than a prophet. This is the one about whom it is written: 'I will send my messenger ahead of you who will prepare your way before you.' I tell you, among those born of women there is no one greater than John; yet the one who is least in the Kingdom of God is greater than he."***

(All the people, even the tax collectors, when they heard Jesus' words, acknowledged that God's way was right, because they had been baptized by John. But the Pharisees and the experts in the law rejected God's purpose for themselves, because they had not been baptized by John.)

In this passage, we find John the Baptist – according to Jesus **"the greatest man born of woman"** under the old covenant – doubting Jesus. (Matthew 11:11) John's circumstance of being in jail and the sense that his days were numbered, made him wonder about Jesus, **"Are you the one who is to come?"** In other words, are you the promised Messiah?

Interestingly, Jesus' answer is not a simple "yes" but He gives definitive evidence of being the Messiah, **"The blind receive sight, the lame walk, those who have leprosy are cleansed, the deaf hear, the dead are raised and good news is preached to the poor."** These same evidences were in Isaiah 61:1-2 – the text for Jesus' first sermon in Nazareth where He announces His Global Spiritual Revolution.

Then Jesus adds a curious ending to His message to John**, "Blessed is anyone who does not stumble on account of me."** (Other translations say "fall away" instead of "stumble.") Here Jesus in essence is saying to John, "I am not the Messiah that you expected – one who eats locust and honey and abstains from bread and wine. But look at what I am doing and this proves from the Scriptures that I am the Messiah." Like John, many people "miss" Jesus and the Kingdom because of preconceived ideas and false traditional doctrines. I was almost one of them! The first time that I came to the Crossroads Church of Christ, I did not like it! After all, the singing was so loud; during the sermon people were yelling "Amen;" there was all the seemingly fake hugging; and church lasted over an hour! Bottom line, the sermon made me feel so uncomfortable and it was so challenging!

Also of note from this passage, when goodhearted people **"heard Jesus' words"** they knew that they were true. Truth rings true! I did return to the Crossroad Church a few weeks later and saw a college student baptized – fully immersed in water! I remember vividly feeling that maybe this was the answer to the emptiness I had felt for a very long time.

Looking back, I grew up in a very traditional and religious Cuban home that was very protective. Even as a young girl of six years old, I did not like to eat vegetables. So I would hide them in my napkin and trained myself to throw up the ones I ate so that my parents would not make me eat any more. One day, my Papá found the hidden peas in my napkin and then I threw up! I said the peas made me sick. Papá answered while holding a spoon, "If you throw up again, you will have to eat your thrown up peas!" Needless to say, I stopped throwing them up and learned to like most vegetables! I also believe I was saved from a life of bulimia!

However particularly during my junior and senior years of high school, bitterness was growing in my heart towards my parents. I was quietly very rebellious and deceitful towards my parents' strict rules of not spending the night at my friends' homes, having a curfew to be home by 11PM on the weekends, and their wanting to know everywhere I was going and whom I was with!

My youngest brother Peter was born in America in 1963. Our family grew with the addition of my two cousins – Maruchi and Javier – who were more like siblings. Their father Francisco, who was my father's older brother by 10 years, was a renowned neurosurgeon who was trained in America. Their family fled Cuba a year after us with only five dollars in my uncle's pocket. They came to Gainesville and lived with us and fortunately "Tío" (Uncle) Francisco quickly landed a job at the University of Florida Shands Hospital. In time, Tío Francisco and "Tía" (Aunt) Margarita were able to buy a house quite near to my family's home so the two Garcia-Bengochea families were together constantly.

Growing up in a larger family with children all about the same age was chaotic, but fun! Mamá was a very strong woman, but we often wore her out with our wrestling, screaming and constant attempts to annoy each other. In response, Mamá involved us in community sports classes such as swimming, golf, ballet and tennis to channel our energies. Our neighbors who helped to "Americanize" us were a high-powered tennis family who had children similar in age to us. We also had wonderful tennis opportunities through this kind family. Due to my parents' expectations for all of us to go to college someday, we attended a great school from kindergarten through high school – P.K. Yonge Developmental Research School. Whenever I needed help in school my parents were there for me. Mamá inspired me to love reading and helped me with my Spanish homework. Papá helped me with my math and science classes. Thanks to their expectations and accountability, they instilled in me a hard work ethic and I achieved straight A's as a student.

I also became super involved in athletics during the late 60's and 70's. During this time there was a tremendous amount of experimentation with drugs. Even at my private high school this was happening and thankfully my parents taught us to stay away from the drug world. Sadly, I deceived my parents and went to a few crazy parties with some friends. At one of these parties, I gave into peer pressure and took one puff of marijuana for my first and only time… I felt really scared and guilty.

My best friends growing up were my older sister Carmen and my first cousin Maruchi. Carmen, who is two years my senior, and I shared a room. We played tennis together almost daily, and we participated in tennis lessons and clinics often at the University of Florida. We were both city champions in tennis for our age groups in singles and doubles and we also went on to play in junior state tournaments. My other closest friend Cynthia, that I had met in nursery school, was in the same class with me from kindergarten to eleventh grade in high school. We shared much of our lives together and she was accepted into an early medical school program where she graduated a year early from high school. I was so happy and proud of her, but I missed her dearly during my senior year.

Even though I had many superficial friendships, I felt really lonely with Carmen and Cynthia away at college. I cried myself to sleep many nights, confused as well as bitter with men. With the heavy influence of the Women's Lib Movement in this university town, I grew to feel very antagonistic and competitive with men verses feeling "liberated." I also felt suppressed in the traditional religious world in which I grew up. To fill the emptiness, I was very involved in my high school and became an officer in student government, captain of the cheerleading squad, and played number one for my high school tennis team.

However, I still felt I could not trust anyone outside my family. My senior year I started dating a guy exclusively. He was a kind young man who I considered my new best friend. We were classmates for several years and had built a great friendship. He was the Student Body President while I served as the Treasurer. He was Homecoming King and I was elected Homecoming Queen. He was a great basketball player and I was a varsity cheerleader for three years. We both inspired each other to academic excellence and enjoyed spending time together. He would give his whole heart while playing tennis with me, even though he knew I could beat him very significantly. As our relationship grew it became more important than anything else in my life.

Though very religious and having an appearance of being successful, I still was not fulfilled. I knew something was missing. One day while driving home alone from my high school tennis practice, I cried out to God, "Please help me! I don't know what I'm doing with my life! Show me or take my life!" During this time, my older sister and I had drifted apart with her being away at college. Yet just a few weeks after this desperate prayer she came home from college on a Sunday evening for dinner, and enthusiastically shared with me and Mamá that she was now involved in a "Bible Church" and wanted us to visit the Crossroads Church of Christ with her.

Ironically, at our family church service earlier that day, the church that my sister was involved in was talked about in a very negative light. Papá was out of town for work; Mamá was pretty upset; and I was very confused with my faith. The following week we went to a Sunday Service with my sister because she begged us to check it out for ourselves. As I shared earlier, the service was actually very uncomfortable for me. The Sunday that I returned and saw a college student baptized, Carmen then shared with me that she was baptized in the same way recently and asked if I wanted to study the Bible with her. Initially, I declined. With my sister living at home over the summer, I could see the changes in her life – more humility, more kindness and more love towards our family. She would ask me how I was doing on a deeper level which made me think more deeply about my purpose in life.

After my graduation from high school, my sister asked me to go to a College Devotional on Friday night with about 100 other college students. I brought my boyfriend with me who was not raised with any faith in God. Surprisingly, I really enjoyed the singing to God, the heartfelt praying, and the informal Bible discussion groups. I felt so much love and positive spiritual energy that I was inspired to start studying the Bible with my sister and two other college friends of hers.

I began learning so much about God in my Bible studies, but I was still very guarded and religiously prideful. I studied the Bible for three months and made a decision to give up my dating relationship because it was not based on a spiritual foundation. Though we never went "all the way" it was impure. Suddenly, there was persecution from our close family members and even from one of our family's church leaders because they did not really understand why I chose to go to this controversial church. It seemed strange to my parents that I was eager to study the Bible every day and to go to this Bible Church more than once a week. None-the-less, I was baptized into Christ on August 8, 1973 at about 9PM – thus finding my purpose!

I'll never forget how much peace, hope and sense of purpose I felt that night. I felt my heart was healed from all my bitterness, selfishness and sins of the heart so I wrote a letter of thanksgiving to God that night that I treasure to this very day. I now knew that my purpose was to help others find spiritual healing through Christ's teachings. My heart was excited and my mind was filled with new dreams to serve God, not knowing exactly what that would mean for my future.

Incredibly, a month after I was baptized, I began attending the University of Florida! I moved into Broward Hall on an all-women's floor and immediately began hosting a weekly Women's Bible Study Group ("Soul Talk") in my dorm room. At the Soul Talk, we would have very open discussions about our lives as we studied a passage of Scripture. Thankfully helping with the "Soul Talk" was Kathy, who as a senior lived on the first floor of my dorm. She became a very dear and helpful sister. Hosting the "Soul Talk" furthered my sense of purpose to help women as I saw many young women on my floor destroying their lives through partying – drinking, drugs and immorality. Encouragingly, several young women on my floor not only became close friends but also true Christians through this outreach my freshman year! Indeed all through that first year of college, God was teaching me so much through the Bible, particularly how to live for Christ with confidence and purity.

CHAPTER
4

This Generation

Luke 7:31-35 – *Jesus went on to say, "To what, then, can I compare the people of THIS GENERATION? What are they like? They are like children sitting in the marketplace and calling out to each other: 'We played the pipe for you, and you did not dance; We sang a dirge, and you did not cry.'*

For John the Baptist came neither eating bread nor drinking wine, and you say, 'He has a demon.' The Son of Man came eating and drinking, and you say, 'Here is a glutton and a drunkard, a friend of tax collectors and sinners.' But wisdom is proved right by all her children."

Jesus begins this section with the questions, *"To what can I compare the people of THIS GENERATION? What are they like?"* He then parallels the ministry of John the Baptist – a preacher who did not eat bread or drink wine – to singing *"a dirge"* where the people *"did not cry."*

In other words, they had no response to the strong warnings from God from John's preaching. The ministry of Jesus – a preacher who ate and drank and thus had the reputation as **"a glutton, drunkard, friend of tax collectors and sinners"** – was compared to the upbeat playing of **"the flute"** but the people **"did not dance."** The more engaging and warm approach by Jesus in preaching the truth likewise yielded no repentance. So in essence, Jesus challenges us that when one does not accept the message of God it is not because of "the style of preaching," but because one is rejecting God's Word! Jesus' words are equally true today. For that generation is "THIS GENERATION!"

We must now pause and consider the plight of women around the world in THIS GENERATION. According to DoSomething.org, one of the largest organizations for young people and social change, here are 10 alarming statistics:

1) Every 90 seconds, a woman dies during pregnancy or childbirth. Most of these deaths are preventable, but due to gender-based discrimination, many women are not given the proper education or care they need.

2) As many as one in four women experience physical or sexual violence during pregnancy.

3) Women make up 80% of all refugees and displaced people. Instruments of genocide such as sexual violence and rape are often directed at women and girls.

4) Women are seldom included in formal peace processes. Women are usually not represented among decision-makers and military leaders, the usual participants in these processes.

5) As of January 2012, women held just 15.1% of all presiding officer posts in governments of the world.

6) More than 16.4 million women in the world have HIV/AIDS.

7) The US government estimates that 600,000 to 800,000 victims (mostly women and children) are trafficked globally each year, and of these 14,500 to 17,500 are trafficked into the United States.

8) Women account for 70% of the population living in absolute poverty (on less than $1.00 a day).

9) Over 60 million girls worldwide are child brides, married before the age of 18.

10) 603 million women live in countries where domestic violence is not yet considered a crime.

These horrifying statistics do not include the destructive power of pornography affecting women and men in THIS GENERATION through the internet. According to *United Families International* – "a public charity devoted to maintaining and strengthening the family as the fundamental unit of society" – the following statistics show this satanic darkness to be saturating society:

1) 12% of the websites on the internet are pornographic. That's almost 25 million sites.

2) Every second over $3 million is spent viewing pornography by over 28,000 viewers.

3) 40 million Americans are regular visitors to porn sites – one in three are women.

4) The worldwide porn industry annual revenues are $4.9 billion.

5) 25% of all search engine requests are pornography related. That is 68 million per day. There are 116,000 searches for "child pornography" per day.

6) The average age at which a child first views pornography online is 11 years old.

7) In America, the least popular day of the year for viewing pornography is Thanksgiving. The most popular day of the week to view pornography is Sunday.

Jesus' way was not just a revolution of social change but also one of individual transformation. When the number of conversions in a city or nation reach a critical mass, this can impact an entire community as seen in Acts 19 during the riot of Ephesus caused by the lack of idol sales. For the individual entering His Kingdom, the difference between the world and His people will be immediately felt.

Making disciples involves confronting and rooting out of an individual both the sins of the flesh and the heart. Jesus taught, **"For it is from within, out of a person's heart, that evil thoughts come – sexual immorality, theft, murder, adultery, greed, malice, arrogance, and folly. All these evils come from inside and defile a person."** (Mark 7:21-23) When the call to repent is individually applied to those seeking to know God then the grace of God can motivate men's attitudes toward women to change and women's attitudes toward men to change. For men, instead of viewing women as "sex objects" this means looking at all women purely, as sisters and daughters of God or potential ones. For women, it often means forgiving the men who have abused or suppressed them – physically or emotionally – to no longer allow bitterness to harden their hearts causing hatred or apathy.

Sometimes the scars of sins against women affect them in their marriages. This is especially true of those women who have been molested as children. I have counseled countless women who find intimacy difficult – even at times revolting – because of past molestation. Many times even Christian women have never revealed the full extent of their abuse. For many, opening up to a trusted and mature woman disciple begins a healing process. Ultimately, it comes down to each Christian woman remembering and embracing the Parable of the Unmerciful Servant. (Matthew 18:23-35) We must forgive as Christ forgave us, or we will not be forgiven. (Colossians 3:13)

Not long ago, a young couple came to Kip and me for help in their marriage. Though at first, it seemed like the primary problem was unresolved conflicts, it did not take long to discover the deep wounds in the young wife from molestation as a child where she viewed even marital sex as "corrupt and worldly." It also came to light that the young man had fallen back into the sins of pornography and masturbation. These serious issues fed on each other further frustrating each spouse. By studying out the Word, daily prayer as a couple, the brother repenting of impurity, and the sister forgiving those who sinned grievously against her, healing has occurred! Today they are quite close in their marriage and are helping other couples find healing through Christ while serving in the fulltime ministry!

Someone once said, "The world is the way it is because the church is the way it is." If the church is to change the world, there must be a motivating vision. This vision is recorded in 1 Timothy 2:3-4, *"God our Savior… wants all people to be saved and to come to a knowledge of the truth."* This passage teaches that it is the will of God to save all people. Therefore, the modern church and each Christian must ask themselves, "Is God's will my will?" From this passage comes the vision of the SoldOut Movement – the evangelization of all nations in THIS GENERATION. Interestingly, a few verses later in 1 Timothy 3:16, Paul records a first century confession of faith that was most likely sung as a hymn:

He appeared in the flesh,
was vindicated by the Spirit,
was seen by angels,
was preached to all nations,
was believed on in the world,
was taken up in glory.

The Book of 1 Timothy is usually dated around 63AD. Therefore, by then – perhaps around 34 years after the church was initiated on the Day of Pentecost in 29AD – the Christians believed the world was evangelized in their generation for they sang, *"was preached to all nations."* This concurs with Paul's words written in 62AD in Colossians 1:23, *"This is the Gospel that you heard and that has been proclaimed to every creature under Heaven…"*

Interestingly, one of the last prophecies of Jesus to the Apostles before His crucifixion also espoused this glorious vision, *"Then you will be handed over to be persecuted and put to death, and you will be hated by all nations because of me… Because of the increase of wickedness, the love of most will grow cold, but the one who stands firm to the end will be saved. And this Gospel of the Kingdom will be preached in the whole world as a testimony to all nations, and then the end will come… Truly I tell you, THIS GENERATION will certainly not pass away until all these things have happened."* (Matthew 24:9-14, 34) Jesus foresees that all nations will hate the Apostles because of their proclamation of the Kingdom. This testimony will be preached *"in the whole world"* and He adds, *"then the end will come."* Most commentators agree *"the end"* of which Jesus speaks is the well-documented destruction by the Romans of the Temple and the entire city of Jerusalem in 70AD. Jesus adds, *"THIS GENERATION will certainly not pass away until all these things have happened"* Jesus believed in the evangelization of the nations in HIS GENERATION.

The church and in fact every disciple must have this same vision to be everything that God desires. This requires so much courage, love and sacrifice and explains why Jesus shares in His vision that *"the love of most will grow cold, but the one who stands firm to the end will be saved."* Women disciples must embrace and hold on to this vision no matter the cost or else they will simply become merely church-goers.

To change the world – to be centered in Jesus' revolution – is a decision that I have had to make at every key juncture in my life. Perhaps one of the most difficult moments of my life occurred in April 2003, when I was 48 years old having dedicated myself for 24 years to the fulltime ministry. At that time, Kip and I were fired from the fulltime ministry in Los Angeles, because we would not compromise on three core convictions: 1) Discipling is a command of God for every Christian and is not optional (Matthew 28:18-20); 2) The movement of God requires a central leader so that disciples will not be *"like sheep without a shepherd,"* as congregational autonomy is not God's plan (Numbers 27:15-18);

and 3) The vision of the evangelization of the nation in THIS GENERATION is God's plan. (1 Timothy 2:3-4)

To understand fully just how devastating our firing was, let me go back in my life's story to June 1, 1979. It was on this date that Kip and I were privileged to begin leading the Lexington Church of Christ. (Three years later, since our congregation moved from the little suburb of Lexington into Downtown Boston, we changed the name to the Boston Church of Christ.) Our first gathering was that Friday night for devotional in Bob and Pat Gempel's living room. Here "30 would-be-disciples" came together determined to build a congregation in which every member – in the vernacular of the times – was "totally committed." Since we obeyed the Scriptures' call for discipling in each member's life, God gave us unprecedented growth. Though the Lexington Church had only seen two baptisms in the previous three years, in our very first year, God blessed the "30" with 103 souls baptized into Christ! The next year 200 were baptized; then the following year 252, and by our fourth year 368 were baptized – more than daily baptisms! (Acts 2:47)

Of note, several of these additions were from such campuses as Harvard, MIT, Northeastern University, Boston University, Boston College, Tufts and U Mass Boston! In time, God allowed us to lead this multiplication of disciples which produced a worldwide family of churches called the Boston Movement. In 1990, we moved to Los Angeles to a relatively new planting that had 154 members. In 1994, we formally adopted the name – the International Churches of Christ (ICOC). By 2001, when we were asked to go on sabbatical because of growing disunity toward our leadership and challenges with our children, the Holy Spirit had built the Los Angeles ICOC to 10,000 disciples! Amazingly, from the "30 would-be disciples" in 1979, by 2001, God's global movement multiplied to 135,000 disciples with 200,000 in attendance on Sundays with almost 400 churches in 171 nations on all six populated continents of the globe. As for being asked to go on sabbatical, some have apologized through the years as they too have learned that most families encounter challenges in raising children during their college years. As of today, we are very close to our three married children and they have blessed us with precious grandchildren.

At the end of one-and-a-half years of sabbatical, we were fired. What really crushed my heart was to learn of the "politics" – power struggle – behind our firing by some who at one time were close friends and brothers. This damaged my faith in God and in men. I became very disillusioned about staying in the ministry. I was very "man-focused" and lost sight of God and His passion *"for all people to be saved."*

At this point, I am so thankful to God that Kip – even though he was hurting severely – kept his faith. When we received the phone call in June 2003 where we were asked to lead the devastated Portland ICOC, I wanted to return to the security of the ensured salary of an occupational therapist. However, Kip – in humility and tears – begged me to stay in the fulltime ministry for just six more months, and if I did not believe that God was calling me then I should return to my OT career. Kip prayed with me every night and even constructed Bible studies that helped me slowly regain my faith.

Quite intriguingly, my broken heart began to heal as I served God through helping the women of the Portland Church. The Scriptures are always true, *"The Lord is close to the brokenhearted and saves those who are crushed in spirit. The righteous person may have many troubles but the Lord delivers him from them all."* (Psalm 34:18) To this day, I am so grateful for the love, mercy and grace extended to Kip and me through the original leaders of the Portland Church – in particular by Nick and Denise Bordieri, Tony and Therese Untalan, Michael and Michele Williamson, Jeremy and Amy Ciaramella, and Jay and Angie Hernandez.

As well, disciples – who shared our core convictions on discipling, central leadership and the evangelization of all nations in THIS GENERATION – began to move to Portland from all over the United States. God gathered disciples from 26 of the 50 states of America! These golden-hearted "remnant"[1] disciples moved hundreds of miles, because they believed the Portland Church was one of the few congregations from what was left of the ICOC movement that still practiced discipling!

Among those that joined were Matt & Helen Sullivan of Fresno, California. They attended the First Portland Jubilee – **The Lord Of The Fellowship** – in June 2004. They were spiritually "awakened" at the Jubilee and decided to move that summer for the spiritual well-being of their three young children and for Matt to follow "his dream" to train fulltime for the ministry. The Sullivans were the first of many to sell their home in order to have the funds to relocate to Portland. They supported themselves through the selling of their home and by Helen working fulltime as a college administrator. Helen and I became best of friends as we had so much in common. In particular, we both came to understand that God called us into the fulltime ministry through our awesome husbands! Later, God blessed their faith as they served fulltime leading the churches in Phoenix, Arizona; Santiago, Chile; and Orlando, Florida! And most inspirationally, later all three of their precious children were baptized as teenagers!

Over the next three years from 2003 to 2006, God built the 25 member Portland Church – through baptisms, restorations and remnant disciples moving in – into almost 500 disciples who were united on the vision of the evangelization of the nations in THIS GENERATION. In October of 2006, God then used this vision to initiate His new movement – the SoldOut Discipling Movement. Sadly, from 2001 to 2006, many in our former fellowship became confused and lukewarm or fell away thus fulfilling Jesus' prophecy that *"the love of most will grow cold."* Indeed, *"Without vision the people perish."* (Proverbs 29:18 KJV)

1.   Remnant in Isaiah 10:20-22 is the survivors of God's people.

CHAPTER
5

An Alabaster Jar of Perfume

Luke 7:36-50 – *When one of the Pharisees invited Jesus to have dinner with him, He went to the Pharisee's house and reclined at the table. A woman in that town who lived a sinful life learned that Jesus was eating at the Pharisee's house, so she came there with an alabaster jar of perfume. As she stood behind Him at His feet weeping, she began to wet His feet with her tears. Then she wiped them with her hair, kissed them and poured perfume on them. When the Pharisee who had invited Him saw this, he said to himself, 'If this man were a prophet, He would know who was touching Him and what kind of woman she is – that she is a sinner.'*

*Jesus answered him, **"Simon, I have something to tell you."** "Tell me teacher," he said. **"Two people owed*** *money to a certain money lender. One owed him five hundred denarii, and the other fifty. Neither of them had the money to pay him back, so he forgave the debts of both. Now which of them will love him more?"* Simon replied, "I suppose the one who had the bigger debt forgiven." "You have judged correctly," Jesus said.

Then He turned toward the woman and said to Simon, *"Do you see this woman? I came into your house. You did not give me any water for my feet, but she wet my feet with her tears and wiped them with her hair. You did not give me a kiss, but this woman from the time I entered, has not stopped kissing my feet. You did not put oil on my head, but she has poured perfume on my feet. Therefore, I tell you, her many sins have been forgiven – as her great love has shown. But whoever has forgiven little loves little."*

Then Jesus said to her, *"Your sins are forgiven."* The other guests began to say among themselves, "Who is this who even forgives sin?" Jesus said to the woman, *"Your faith has saved you; go in peace."*

There is much confusion about which "Mary" is the focus of Jesus' praise in this passage. John 11:2 clearly identifies the **"sinful woman"** of Luke 7 as Mary of Bethany. **"This Mary, whose brother Lazarus now lays sick, was the same one who poured perfume on the Lord and wiped His feet with her hair."** The confusion is cleared up even more so when the passage is translated as **"a woman who HAD lived a sinful life."** (1984 NIV) So Jesus was challenging a social stigma found in all societies in all centuries that a bad reputation often continues to be held over a person's head even after they had changed… but not so with Jesus! Notice as well that Jesus tells the story of two individuals who **"HAD"** their debts forgiven. (Luke 7:41-42) So it is implied that Simon **"HAD"** been forgiven and the sinful woman **"HAD"** been forgiven, but their responses to Jesus were drastically different.

Another account of this incident is in Matthew 26:6-13. Of note is verse six, **"While Jesus was in Bethany in the home of Simon the Leper…"** Jesus most likely had cured this Simon – Simon the Pharisee – of leprosy and that is why he is called Simon the Leper in Matthew's Gospel. One presumes that he is not addressed as Simon the Leper in the account by Luke, the doctor, because Simon had been cured! (Colossians 4:14) Another interesting account of the **"sinful woman"** and Simon the Leper is in Mark 14:1-9. Of note are verses four through nine, **"Some of those present were saying indignantly to one another, 'Why this waste of perfume? It could have been sold for more than a year's wages and the money given to the poor.' And they rebuked her harshly. 'Leave her alone,' said Jesus. 'Why are you bothering her? She has done a beautiful thing to me. The poor you will always have with you, and you can help them any time you want. But you will not always have me. She did what she could. She poured perfume on my body beforehand to prepare for my burial. Truly I tell you, wherever the gospel is preached throughout the world, what she has done will also be told, in memory of her.'"** Here we learn that Mary's gratitude is so profound in Jesus' mind that her unique act of devotion will be remembered as **"the Gospel is preached throughout the world."** Therefore, from this Scripture, we can conclude again that Jesus did intend for the Gospel to be preached to the entire world!

In John 12:1-8, Judas – the Apostle who betrays Jesus – was the one who objected about the money being wasted by this woman with the perfume. In verse six the Bible says, **"[Judas] did not say this because he cared about the poor but because he was a thief; as keeper of the money bag, he used to help himself to what was put into it."** Relatively few events are in all four Gospels.

So the fact that Mary's anointing of Jesus is indeed detailed in all four Gospels, should make us look all the more closely at this very moving event.

The heart of the passage in Luke centers on Mary – *"a woman who HAD lived a sinful life"* – realizing just how much she had been forgiven. Luke details a very stark contrast between Simon's and Mary's responses to Jesus. Yes, from a "counting of total sins perspective," perhaps Simon was more "righteous," but this perspective is exactly what Jesus was teaching against. Jesus tells a story where a man forgives one person of a debt of 500 denarii and the other person is forgiven a debt of only 50 denarii. (According to Matthew 20:2, a Roman denarius is a day's wage.) Jesus asks Simon, *"Now which of them will love him more?"* Sensing that Jesus was going after a counter intuitive response, Simon hesitantly answers, *"I suppose the one who had the bigger debt forgiven."* Jesus then gently confronts Simon on the difference of his and Mary's approach to Him, which reveals the heart.

In essence, Mary was ultra-humble and grateful literally to the point of tears, while Simon was somewhat stoic in his welcoming of Jesus. Then Jesus lays out the truth, *"Therefore, I tell you, her many sins have been forgiven – as her great love has shown. But whoever has been forgiven little loves little."* The teaching that Jesus was giving to Simon is that each person should not compare how little they have sinned in comparison to others, but each of us needs to genuinely feel that we have been forgiven much. Therefore, we will "love Jesus much," just like Mary!

Similarly, Paul expresses this same intense gratitude in 1 Corinthians 15:9-10, *"For I am the least of the Apostles and do not even deserve to be called an Apostle, because I persecuted the church of God. But by the grace of God I am what I am, and His grace to me was not without effect. No, I worked harder than all of them – yet not I but the grace of God that was with me."* We learn that Paul felt he worked harder than all the "rest of the Apostles" not because he felt he was "better," but because Paul saw how sinful he was in persecuting the church! So we learn from Mary and Paul that our appreciation of how very much we have been forgiven is directly proportional to how vigorously we serve Him!

So no matter how righteous we may feel "in comparison to others" each of us needs to see how undeserving we are of any forgiveness. Each of us has been *"forgiven much"* and our lives reveal if this is our heart's conviction.

As I grow older in the Lord, my awareness of my own sinfulness has vastly grown. In fact, if you would have asked me if I was a selfish person at baptism, I might have honestly said, "Yes, but not as much as my peers and the other members of my family." However, now I see just how selfish I am! After all, selfishness is the root of all sin. And my selfishness takes so, so many forms: self-absorbed, self-centered, self-conscious, self-critical, self-righteous, self-reliant, self-pitying, self-indulgent, self-important, self-doubt, self-deceived, self-serving, and when I am doing very poorly even self-sufficient… In other words, I want to take my life into my own hands and not be surrendered to the *"race marked out for [me]."* (Hebrews 12:1-2)

So interestingly, since I was four years old until I graduated from college, I lived in the comfortable little city of Gainesville, Florida. In marrying Kip – thus God calling me into the ministry – I have had to crucify self in moving so many times and traveling to plant churches in dangerous places. In particular, I remember the summer of 1989. Kip and I – accompanied by our children who were eight, six and four years old – were used by God to plant the Metro Manila Church in the Philippines and the Bangkok Church in Thailand. Then we led the Cairo Church in Egypt immediately following the governmental persecution that expelled from Egypt all seven Americans on the original mission team for "converting Egyptians to Christianity." I gratefully – *"yet in weakness and fear, and with much trembling"* for our safety – went to each of these three cities because I realized how much I had been forgiven and wanted women in each of these places to have what I had in God's Kingdom! (1 Corinthians 2:1-2)

The '89 missionary journey was also riveting as in the Philippines we confronted false Christianity; in Thailand, we daily saw the devastating effects of the idolatry in Buddhism; and in Cairo, we encountered the suppression by Islam. In the city of Metro Manila, I saw the abject poverty of the third world with 75,000 street children, as well as the moms that used their children to beg for them. I'll always remember that our first convert – a delightful but shy college girl – had 30 visitors out at the Sunday service following her baptism! Truly, she exemplifies the heart of Mary who **"loved much!"** In Bangkok, I saw the overt sex-trafficking as it was said at the time that "one out of every six women is or was in prostitution." Our very first baptism in Bangkok was a young woman that God graciously delivered from this dreadful life! In Cairo, the Egyptian women seemed so suppressed. But in the church, the young women disciples were so joyful and full of dreams to serve God!

So sad in retrospect, Kip was heavily criticized even by fellow leaders for even sending a mission team to Cairo. Moreover, in the mind of these overly cautious critics, this was validated eight months later when the seven Americans were ingloriously "kicked out" of the country never to return, even though these eight courageous members of this mission team had 23 baptisms in eight months! (One member of the team was Egyptian and therefore was not expelled from his homeland.) On top of this criticism – again inside the movement and even from a few family members – Kip and I were heavily criticized for taking our children with us to these third world cities endangering their lives. We did take precautions such as getting immunization shots, carefully selecting where we lived, not drinking tap water, and closely following the advice of Christian nationals. Yes, each of the members of our family took turns getting intense stomach sicknesses, but overall, these days had a tremendous positive impact on our children. They grew up aware of the poverty, the plight of women, and the different value systems in third world countries. In others words, our efforts for Christ made our children much more globally aware, much more compassionate, and much less "spoiled" as Americans. These challenging times transformed Kip and me from "American Christians" to "Global Disciples!"

A very essential principle of missions is given by Paul in 2 Thessalonians 3:3, **"But the Lord is faithful, and He will strengthen and protect you from the evil one."** God orchestrates our protection in many miraculous ways! One of them is through direct intervention in the decisions of world leaders, for that is why we are called to pray **"for all those in authority."** (1 Timothy 2:1-4) We saw this happen in South Africa after we sent the multiracial mission team into this nation in 1986, shortly afterward God struck down the law of Apartheid! A similar event occurred shortly after we led the mission team of 17 into Moscow in 1991. The failed coup by the communist hardliners led to religious freedom for the first time in 70 years thus allowing the evangelization of the 15 former Soviet Union nations. Most notably in our first year in Moscow, God gave us 850 baptisms!

Another way that God protected us was through the wisdom of disciples and non-Christian "family and friends" of influence similar to those who "protected" Paul. (Acts 19:31; 23:16-22; 28:10) Quite fond in my memory is our dear brother John Beshai – the Egyptian lawyer converted in Boston not long before we sent out the Cairo Mission Team in 1988. John used his influence as the Vice President of the Sadat Peace Foundation to have Kip and our family always escorted "around customs" by one of the Egyptian senators! During our month in Cairo, John remained steadfastly by our side as well as helping to evangelize his beloved people. This gave me tremendous peace and a growing conviction that God brings people into our lives to help us in accomplishing His purposes and the dream of the evangelization of the nations in this generation. In 2011, John courageously joined the new movement. On September 1, 2013, John passed on into glory! Ultimately, our willingness to "go anywhere" allowed the Spirit to plant and to sustain churches of true disciples where there previously were none.

Though the nature of our missionary journey in the summer of 1989 was very sobering, there were many times of fun and laughter! There were the crazy daily downpours in Manila where we were drenched in literally less than a minute, as well as one particularly humorous event about which the children tease Kip to this day! The entire Manila Mission Team was staying at the old and the rather rundown Gilarmi Apartments, when one night at 4AM or so Kip woke up yelling, "Something's in my ear!" I comfortingly said, "Babe you're just having a bad dream. Go back to sleep…" But Kip kept insisting, "No! No! It's like the movie *The Wrath of*

Khan something's gone into my ear!" I could not see anything, but Kip asked me to pour rubbing alcohol into his ear. As I carefully poured the alcohol into his ear, lo and behold a bloody cockroach popped out! Early the next morning typical of Kip making sure the family was safe, he bought and then sprayed our little apartment with two giant cans of Raid Roach Killer!

Another amusing experience was eating foods that at first did not satisfy our American palates! In Manila on most mornings, we would drink the rather tart Filipino calamansi juice instead of the American concentrated orange juice. Now Kip and I prefer calamansi juice, not to mention the fresh, sweet mangos and bananas of the Philippines! At breakfast and sometimes again at night, the Galarmi Apartment would serve congee – a chicken broth with rice and onions. In Thailand, we enjoyed pineapple rice, chicken satay and the tropical fruit called pomelo! In Cairo, we all enjoyed a steady diet of pita bread with hummus and baba ganoush! The children learned to be opened minded about ethnic foods, and also not to be so "picky" about what was put before them to eat.

The alabaster jar of perfume of Mary was worth a year's wages. Our lives are even more precious. So how do we spend our lives? For Kip and me, we remain inspired by Mary ***"who did what she could."*** One of my favorite devotional songs is *I'll Do My Best!* When translated and sung in Spanish it became *Doy Lo Mejor* which literally means – *"I give my best!"* This is my prayer that every day I will give my best to God because of "how much I have been forgiven!"

CHAPTER
6

The Three

Luke 8:1-3 – *After this, Jesus traveled about from one town and village to another, proclaiming the good news of the Kingdom of God. The Twelve were with Him, and also some women who had been cured of evil spirits and diseases: Mary (called Magdalene) from whom seven demons had come out; Joanna the wife of Chuza, the manager of Herod's household; Susanna; and many others. These women were helping to support them out of their own means.*

It is my conviction that God "reveals" in the Scriptures the vital concepts of the multiplication of disciples only to those that are earnestly striving to follow His plan for Global Spiritual Revolution. (Matthew 13:11) In fact, for years I overlooked the magnitude of implications for women's ministry from this passage. These three simple verses have inspired me to grasp and to study out just how essential women leaders were to Jesus' ministry!

In the Message Bible this remarkable passage reads: *"[Jesus] continued according to plan, traveled to town after town, village after village, preaching God's Kingdom, spreading the Message. The Twelve were with Him. There were also some women in their company who had been healed of various evil afflictions and illnesses: Mary, the one called Magdalene, from whom seven demons had gone out; Joanna, wife of Chuza, Herod's manager; and Susanna – along with many others who used their considerable means to provide for the company."*

Women were traveling with Jesus as part of His *"company"* of disciples spreading the message. These women were also the ones financially supporting Jesus and *"the company"* of disciples. There are three significant women that were mentioned here: Mary called Magdalene, Joanna and Susanna. These women were Jesus' "inner circle of women leaders" paralleling Jesus' "inner circle of the three Apostles" – Peter, James and John. Interestingly, the inner circle of Apostles – well documented and discussed in most books on discipling – are mentioned for the first time later in Luke 8:51. Intriguingly, in the midst of the Women's Elevation Section of Luke, the triumvirate of women leaders were highlighted first! This concept of Jesus' women's leadership group was so revolutionary for the Jewish world… and even Christendom today!

The "inner circle of Apostles" – Peter, James and John – is spoken about at three very key junctures in Jesus' ministry. The first is witnessing the resurrection from the dead of Jairus' daughter. The second occurs on the Mount of Transfiguration. (Matthew 17:1; Mark 9:2; Luke 9:28) And the last instance is during the heart-wrenching hour in the Garden of Gethsemane, where Jesus gets completely open only with the Three. *"He took Peter and the two sons of Zebedee along with Him, and began to be sorrowful and troubled. Then He said to them, 'My soul is overwhelmed with sorrow to the point of death.'"* (Matthew 26:37; Mark 14:33) It is difficult to be totally open in a huge group of 12; so the "inner three" provided a friendship for sharing His deepest concerns and even fears. No one would deny the closeness and specialness of Jesus' relationship with "the Three."

Therefore, we must assume that there was a pure but special relationship with the three women – a relationship that was preparing them for leadership.

It should be noted as well that in every list of Apostles, some names are interchanged, but Peter is always mentioned first. (Matthew 10:2-4; Mark 3:16-19; Luke 6:13-16; John 21:2; Acts 1:13) As well, Peter is listed first when the Gospel writers mention the Three Apostles though James and John are interchanged. This same "first on the list" dynamic is found with Mary Magdalene. In every list of women involved in Jesus' ministry – except when Jesus was talking to His mother from the cross – Mary Magdalene is listed first! (Matthew 27:56, 61; 28:1; Mark 15:40, 47; 16:1; Luke 8:2; 24:10)

No doubt, Peter is the leader of the Apostles and all the disciples in the days after Jesus' ascension both before and after the Day of Pentecost. He leads the 120 in selecting Judas' replacement (Acts 1:15-26); Peter is the only "highlighted preacher" on the Day of Pentecost (Acts 2:14); Peter gives the **"keys to the Kingdom"** to the Jews (Acts 2:38-41); Peter speaks to the Sanhedrin (Acts 4:5-22); Peter gathers the entire church for prayer (Acts 4:23-31); Peter is used by God to discipline Ananias and Sapphira; Peter with John lays hands on the Samaritan Christians; Peter gives the **"keys to the Kingdom"** to the Gentiles (Acts 10); and though James the half-brother of Jesus is leading the Jerusalem Church, Peter is the only Apostle to speak up at the pivotal Jerusalem Council. Jesus "groomed" Peter to lead. Given the lists of women, we may safely assume the same of Mary Magdalene.

Though Mary Magdalene was the leader of the women leaders, the same intimacy as Peter to Jesus would have been improper. Jesus realized that He needed to treat women with absolute purity, so except for the resurrection – of which Mary Magdalene was given the incredible honor to be the first witness – Jesus most likely worked through the three women leaders to disciple all the other women who followed Him.

It should be noted that most rabbis of that day only had male students. Jesus was radically different! He welcomed women to sit at His feet (Luke 10:38-41), as well as to watch Him work with people so they too could "follow Him" – imitate Him! That Jesus was a Rabbi who selected women as well as men to teach is undeniable, because when Mary Magdalene sees Jesus after his resurrection she calls Him **"Rabboni"** — my great teacher. The Gospel record need not detail the women's ministry because it was parallel and in submission to the Apostles' ministry. There was no need of a "female Messiah" because Jesus died for all men and all women of the world and then gave the same plan of discipleship for men and women to reach the entire world: ***"Therefore go and make disciples of all nations, baptizing them in the name of the Father and of the Son and of the Holy Spirit, and teaching them to obey everything I have commanded you…"*** (Matthew 28:19-20)

This principle of women leading women is clearly seen in Paul's directives to the Evangelist Titus on how to disciple an entire congregation. ***"You must teach what is in accord with sound doctrine. Teach the older men to be temperate, worthy of respect, self-controlled, and sound in faith, in love and in endurance. Likewise teach the older women to be reverent in the way they live, not to be slanders or addicted to much wine, but to teach what is good. Then they can train the younger women to love their husbands and children, to be self-controlled and pure, to be busy at home, to be kind and to be subject to their husbands, so that no one will malign the Word of God. Similarly, encourage the young men to be self-controlled. In everything set them an example by doing what is good. In your teaching show integrity, seriousness and soundness of speech that cannot be condemned…"*** (Titus 2:1-7 NIV 1984) In these ***"sound doctrine"*** directives, the Evangelist is to work with the older men, older women and the younger men of the congregation. The older women are to ***"train the younger women."*** This is protective for the Evangelist and the young women. Most likely, the Evangelist is not going to be attracted to an "older woman." The same cannot be said of the more attractive and emotionally vulnerable young sisters. How many ministers have not followed these Scriptures and fallen into impurity and immorality with younger women who may have genuinely come to the male ministers for spiritual help and the minister is trying to provide help goodheartedly but close emotional bonds are built and impure temptations ensnare him.

Paul himself adhered to this principle. This is most likely seen when Paul writes to the Roman Church, *"Greet Priscilla and Aquila my co-workers in Christ Jesus. They risked their lives for me. Not only I but all the churches of the Gentiles are grateful to them..."* (Romans 16:3-4) It would have been most unusual in that day – and even in our day – for a married woman to have been listed before her husband unless there was a more prominent role that she fulfilled than her husband. Priscilla led the women of Paul's ministry when she and her husband worked side-by-side with Paul.

Very parallel to this was the early years of the Boston Church. In 1984, I had just given birth to our third child in four years with our second child needing back surgery. Since I needed so much time to focus on meeting our family's needs, it was decided by Kip and me with Bob and Pat Gempel – our best friends and one of the two Elder Couples for the Boston Church – that Kip would lead the church (and the movement) while Pat trained me and the other young women leaders. I learned so much from Pat as she was a very spiritual disciple, an excellent wife, and a tremendous mother of grown up children. She was 14 years older than Kip, 15 years older than me. As well, she was a gifted leader as she served as a vice president in her consulting firm – Arthur D. Little. Pat taught me to *"speak the truth in love"* (Ephesians 4:15) yet to never complain, *"to set about [my] work vigorously... to watch over [all] the affairs of [my] household"* (Proverbs 31: 17, 27), and *"to [deeply] love my husband and children."* (Titus 2:4) One quick note of encouragement to all the moms: Biblically, according to this passage in Titus 2, if your children are at home, you are still a "young woman!"

I will always treasure the life-saving power of older women discipling younger women through God using Pat literally to save our second son, Sean's life when he was still in my womb! I was almost three months pregnant and Olivia was just a 14 month old baby, Kip was out of town speaking and helping in a church, when I started bleeding quite a lot on a Thursday. The next morning on a Friday I went to my OBGYN doctor to get checked out and he gave me a quick check-up and matter-of-factly told me I was having a miscarriage, which many women have and scheduled me for a "D&C" procedure where they clear out your whole female area with the "dead" baby.

I came home crying and praying for God to save this baby and immediately called Pat at her work. She answered and quickly called her sister, Donna who was a Christian and an ultrasound technician which was at this time a very new medical procedure that I had never had with my smooth pregnancy with Olivia. Donna squeezed me in that afternoon for an ultrasound and arranged for me to see and get a second opinion from the doctor for whom she worked. Miraculously, our baby Sean (who we had not named yet) was fine with a strong heartbeat, but I had a small hole in my placenta that was causing the bleeding so she ordered me to complete bed rest to let the hole heal up. Pat, Donna and I all cried at the wonderful news and I immediately canceled my DNC and found a new doctor to deliver our baby! Again God used my "spiritual Mom" and sister to help me through this traumatic time and literally saved Sean's life! Of course, I called Kip to share with him how God used our spiritual family to help me and our future baby, Sean!

As mentioned earlier in 1990, God moved our family to Los Angeles to begin leading the newly planted church. At that time, I once again joyfully led the Women's Ministry – both in LA and around the world – alongside Kip. Pat had graciously served in this role for several years while our children were young, and I will be eternally grateful to Pat, as she is my spiritual Mom!

In considering the 12 Apostles, and even more so the three inner circle Apostles and the three women leaders who accompanied Jesus – Mary Magdalene, Joanna and Susanna – the principle of focusing on the few is revealed. This principle is essential for multiplication. It is also equally essential to meet all the needs of these escalating numbers of disciples. In Exodus 18, Jethro – Moses' father in law – saw the long lines of those who were seeking Moses' direction. Jethro tells

Moses, *"What you are doing is not good. You and these people that come to you will only wear yourselves out. The work is too heavy for you; you cannot handle it alone. Listen now to me and I'll give you some advice, and may God be with you… [Select] capable men from all the people – men who fear God, trustworthy men who hate dishonest gain – and appoint them as officials over thousands, hundreds, fifties and tens. Have them serve as judges for the people at all times, but have them bring every difficult case to you; the simple cases they can decide themselves. That will make your load lighter, because they will share it with you. If you do this and God so commands, you will be able to stand the strain, and the people will go home satisfied."* (Exodus 18:17-23) Consider that focusing on a few is something that *"God so commands."* No matter how large our women's ministry becomes we can meet every sister's needs and keep "our sanity" if we focus on training a *"trustworthy"* few.

It is not at all surprising that we again see this principle in Paul's ministry. He challenges the young Evangelist Timothy to do the same. *"And the things that you have heard me say in the presence of many witnesses entrust to reliable people who will also be qualified to teach others."* (2 Timothy 2:2) Here we once again see the principle of focusing on a few. We also can see four generations of discipleship: Paul, Timothy, *"reliable people,"* and *"others."* This is how the multiplication of disciples and the multiplication of leaders to lead them takes place. This explains why Jesus focused on Mary Magdalene, Joanna and Susanna. Through these few women, He could disciple more women leaders to disciple the ever growing number of women disciples.

Let's consider why these "three women" were hand-picked by Jesus. Luke 8:2 tells us that these women *"had been cured of evil spirits and diseases."* So in fact, we learned that of all the thousands of women that Jesus met in His ministry, Jesus chose these three and a few others to heal and be in His company. They must have been very, very grateful for Jesus personally changing their lives.

Perhaps the most grateful was Mary Magdalene as she had *"seven demons come out"* of her! In the four Gospels, Mary Magdalene is specifically mentioned

15 times if you include the references in John 20:11 and John 20:16 where she is addressed merely as "Mary" without the designation of where she was from – Magdala, a city on the southwest coast of the Sea of Galilee. The prominence of her name beyond most of the Apostles begs us to consider that indeed she was the prominent woman leader for Jesus.

As for Joanna, she was married to Chuza, the manager of the King of Galilee Herod Antipas's household. As the wife of a noted court official, she would have had the means to travel as well as to contribute to supporting Jesus and His **"company."** Most likely, Chuza permitted her travels out of gratefulness of Jesus curing his wife.

The mention of Joanna's husband should remind us of another reason that women's discipleship is not as prominent or as straight forward as the discipleship of men in Scripture. As we know in the Bible, **"wives should submit to their husbands in everything"** except disobeying the Lord. (Ephesians 5:24) That said, for a woman to please God and to please her husband at the same time can be complicated. Even Paul alludes to this when he writes, **"But a married man is concerned about the affairs of this world – how he can please his wife – and his interests are divided... [as well] a married woman is concerned about... how she can please her husband."** (1 Corinthians 7:32-34) Joanna shows that a woman can be an effective and contributing married disciple. What a tremendous help Joanna must have been guiding married women on how to deal with being married especially to non-Christians, which many infer that she was. Joanna's faithfulness is confirmed as she was one of the women who reported to the Eleven that Jesus was risen! (Luke 24:10)

As for Susanna, we know little except that she was healed and chosen by Jesus. She too helped to support Jesus' ministry. So like Joanna, Susanna must have been independently wealthy. Her lack of "credentials" may in fact be her inspiration to most of us! After all, **"Not many of you were wise by human standards; not many were influential; not many were of noble birth... so that no one may boast before Him."** (1 Corinthians 1:26-29)

One of the most rewarding aspects of women's ministry is raising-up and appointing new Women Ministry Leaders. Through much prayer and counsel, Kip and I are presently focused on discipling 12 very reliable and capable couples who are devoted to the Lord, to each other, and to the evangelization of the nations in this generation. Since each couple has an evangelistic charge of a sector of the world, we call these couples – World Sector Leaders. Combined these sectors of the world span the entire globe – to which God has called His people to **"go and make disciples of all nations."** (Matthew 28:19-20) These dearest of friends include: Tim and Lianne Kernan, Andrew and Patrique Smellie, Cory and Jee Blackwell, Kyle and Joan Bartholomew, Matt and Helen Sullivan, Raul and Lynda Moreno, Michael and Michele Williamson, Joe and Kerry Willis, Oleg and Elena Sirotkin, Michael and Sharon Kirchner, Nick and Denise Bordieri and Tony and Therese Untalan. The focus of my discipling is to meet the needs of these women, some of whom are like sisters and others are daughters to me. Some of them do not have children, while others have children and grandchildren! Beyond their family responsibilities, each of these precious sisters has the ministry charge to raise up more Women Ministry Leaders, to meet the needs of their women in their local congregations, and through multiplying disciples to evangelize the women of their world sector.

The need of the hour is for more Marys, Joannas and Susannas! Women who are totally devoted to following Jesus through being trained and training other **"reliable"** and **"capable"** women who will train still others. Out of gratefulness that their lives are healed, the modern Marys, Joannas and Susannas must sacrifice "whatever it takes" to support and sustain the ministry of Jesus.

CHAPTER
7

*Three Secrets of
the Kingdom*

Luke 8:4-10 – *While a large crowd was gathering and people were coming to Jesus from town after town, He told this parable: "A farmer went out to sow his seed. As he was scattering the seed, some fell along the path; it was trampled on, and the birds ate it up. Some fell on rocky ground, and when it came up, the plants withered because they had no moisture. Other seed fell among thorns, which grew up with it and choked the plants. Still other seed fell on good soil. It came up and yielded a crop, a hundred times more than was sown."*

When He said this, He called out, "Whoever has ears to hear, let them hear." His disciples asked Him what this parable meant. He said, "The knowledge of the secrets of the Kingdom of God has been given to you, but to others I speak in parables, so that, though seeing they may not see; though hearing, they may not understand."

SECRET ONE
-THE SECRET OF A NOBLE HEART-

Luke 8:11-18 – *"This is the meaning of the parable: The seed is the Word of God. Those along the path are the ones who hear, and then the devil comes and takes away the Word from their hearts, so that they may not believe and be saved. Those on the rocky ground are the ones who receive the Word with joy when they hear it, but they have no root. They believe for a while, but in the time of testing they fall away. The seed that fell among thorns stands for those who hear, but as they go on their way they are choked by life's worries, riches and pleasures, and they do not mature. But the seed on good soil stands for those with a noble and good heart, who hear the Word, retain it, and by persevering produce a crop."*

"No one lights a lamp and hides it in a clay jar or puts it under a bed. Instead, they put it on a stand, so that those who come in can see the light. For there is nothing hidden that will not be disclosed, and nothing concealed that will not be known or brought out into the open. Therefore consider carefully how you listen. Whoever has will be given more; whoever does not have, even what they think they have will be taken from them."

God has secrets! Disciples do not! When the disciples asked Jesus the meaning of the Parable of the Soils, He shared, *"The knowledge of the secrets of the Kingdom of God has been given to you, but to others I speak in parables, so that, 'though seeing they may not see; though hearing they may not understand.'"* Jesus quotes Isaiah 6:9 because this is an eternal principle of God. Though the Word is *"Spirit and truth,"* God "cloaks" the truth in secrecy so that it can only be understood by those who are seeking Him with all their hearts. I so appreciate my parents giving me a foundational faith in God and His Word by taking our family to mass (church services) almost every weekend, as well as on the holy days such as Ash Wednesday. I heard the Word of God read at each of these services, but it had little or no impact on how I lived my life. I simply did not "get it!" As the above Scripture says, I did *"not understand."* In truth, I did not want to understand. The Bible seemed boring and irrelevant to me.

However, what are the real reasons that I did not want to understand, particularly in high school? The answer lies in the Parable of the Soils. In this remarkable parable, Jesus has us envisioning a farmer – a sower – walking through his field with a pouch of seeds on each hip. As the farmer takes a step, he reaches his right hand into the left seed bag and flings a handful of seeds into the air. He takes another step, his left hand grabs a handful of seeds from the right side pouch, and then he flings these seeds into the air. And this process is repeated until the whole field is planted. Consequently, the seeds indeed land on different types of soils!

The farmer is God or a Christian. The seed is the Word of God. The soils are the hearts of people. Jesus, the best preacher who ever lived, taught in such a way in this parable that every person who has ever heard it is one of these soils; as He said, *"Whoever has ears to hear, let them hear."* Indeed, we all have ears!

The first soil actually was not even a part of the field. After being tossed into the air, the seed *"fell along the path."* Jesus says that this seed *"was trampled on"* – in other words – it was treated with no regard. Then *"the birds ate it up!"* It did not even penetrate the heart of the listener, because *"the devil comes and takes away the Word from their hearts so they may not believe and be saved."* One of the devil's greatest deceptions is that he is not real. Some people genuinely believe that Satan is just a myth like Santa Claus or the Easter Bunny! This was me! Because I accepted humanistic thinking in high school, I not only did not believe in the devil, but I considered parts of the Bible – such as the creation account in Genesis and many of the Old Testament miracles – to be absurd. I was so confused, because I did believe in Jesus' miracles!

Jesus tells us why we are confused, *"Why is my language not clear to you? [Why are you confused?] Because you are unable to hear what I say. You belong to your father, the devil, and you want to carry out your father's desires... not holding to the truth, for there is no truth in him. When he lies, he speaks his native language, for he is a liar and the father of lies. Yet because I tell you the truth, you do not believe me!"* (John 8:43-45) I was confused because I wanted to carry out "my" desires, which I now alarmingly understand to be the devil's desires. I wanted to keep secret my fears, my doubts and my sins such as deceit, rebellion, worry and impurity with my boyfriend. Even in regards to my impurity, I rationalized my sin as being ok since we always had our cloths on.

Disciples must not be naïve; Satan is alive and well and quite powerful! We are in an intense spiritual battle for our souls and the souls of all mankind! Jesus shares this parable, *"When a strong man, fully armed, guards his own house, his possessions are safe. But when someone stronger attacks and overpowers him, he takes away the armor in which the man trusted and divides up his plunder."* (Luke 11:21-22) To the surprise of some, the strong man is Satan. His possessions are the souls of men and women. A Christian becomes more powerful than Satan when one has the Holy Spirit, and so one is able to "steal" souls back from Satan through their salvation. If someone has ever stolen something you value, most of us get very upset and mad. This is exactly Satan's response when someone is baptized and becomes a sold-out disciple! Jesus says in Revelation, *"[Satan] is filled with fury... [and is] enraged... and went off to wage war against... those who keep God's commands and hold fast their testimony about Jesus."* (Revelation 12:12, 17) Satan is at war with disciples as individuals as well as collectively as Jesus' church.

The second soil is the rocky ground where the seed fell and grew, but it quickly withered. These individuals *"receive the Word with joy when they hear it, but*

they have no root. They believe for a while, but in the time of testing they fall away." Persecution is absolutely going to happen! Paul writes, **"In fact, everyone who wants to live a godly life in Christ Jesus will be persecuted."** (2 Timothy 3:12) If you are not being persecuted, then perhaps you are not living a godly life, which includes preaching the Word.

Perhaps the most widespread and damaging persecution for disciples comes from the internet that is full of half-truths and lies from godless people, as well as fallen away disciples who are justifying their departure from **"life and [or] doctrine."** (1 Timothy 4:16) Since the road is narrow, persecutors often use emotionally charged words such as cult, fanatics, brainwashed and love-bombing in their attacks. In the same way Jesus was attacked with emotionally charged words**: "glutton and a drunkard, a friend of tax collectors and sinners"** (Luke 7:34); **"Samaritan and demon-possessed"** (John 8:48); **"raving mad"** (John 10:20); and even **"Beelzabul the prince of demons"** (Luke 11:15)! On the other hand, the charge of being "divisive in families" Jesus fully embraced. (Matthew 10:35-38; Luke 12:51-53)

During the 1980's in Boston and throughout the 1990's while we lived in Los Angeles, Kip, I and the Boston Movement (in 1994 officially called the International Church of Christ) were heavily attacked and persecuted by the press and the television media. Among the more twisted and damaging were: the *Boston Globe* article – *O Come All Ye Faithful* (1986); from the Mainline Church of Christ Flavil Yeakley's book – *The Discipling Dilemma* (1988); from the expensive deprogrammer Steve Hassan's article – *Combating Cult Mind Control* (1988); the infamous *TIME* Article by Richard Ostling – *Keepers Of The Flock* (1992); and from the denominational world, Randy Frame's Christianity Today article – *Church Growth: The Cost Of Discipleship* (1997)!

In addition, particularly throughout the 1990's, the television media on such shows as *ABC News 20/20* falsely tried to portray our church as a cult. Some networks such as the Canadian Broadcast News were so aggressive that they set-up cameras 15 feet away from our house. One woman reporter was so hostile, when I said that Kip was not home, even pushed her way through our kitchen door to try to interview Kip. I calmly but firmly said, "I know that you're just doing your job, but please leave our home right now as we have young children!" A week later in New York City where we were speaking, she followed us through the lobby of our hotel and cornered Kip and me in an elevator with a camera man. An older woman told the reporter (maybe a little too loudly), "Get off this elevator and leave these young people alone!" I felt so much hostility and disrespect from this reporter who was trying to sensationalize that we were "evil cult leaders!" It did make me pray all the harder!

Throughout the years, Kip has received several death threats. On one occasion, a very unstable person even threatened the lives of our children and me. My first experience of this hateful persecution occurred in Charleston, Illinois just a few months after the very sad Jim Jones mass murder-suicide of 909 individuals of the Peoples Temple in Jonestown, Guyana on November 18, 1978. Heartbreaking to me, the local Charleston newspaper – *The Times-Courier* – ran seven straight days of negative articles on the Heritage Chapel Church of Christ being a cult and paralleling Kip to Jim Jones. At this time, a mother of one of our recently baptized college girls – after meeting with me and one of our elders Brother Wayne Geiling one afternoon – came to our Midweek Service with a gun threatening to kill Kip. Fortunately, Kip was again out of town preaching! The older men in the church escorted her out and called the police!

It hurts so much to hear the false charges against the ones I so love. However, these trials have made me appreciate Jesus even more as He was perfect but still was persecuted and martyred for changing the world! I have learned to surrender my fears about Kip's and our children's safety and rely on God's protection. Truly, ***"The Lord is my rock, my fortress and my deliverer… in whom I take refuge… I call to the Lord, who is worthy of praise, and [my family] is saved from [those who try to harm us.]"*** (Psalm 18:2-3)

One sad story about the potentially negative impact of persecution (that ends happily) is about my beloved sister Sharon Kirchner. Sharon was baptized into

Christ while attending University of Missouri in the fall of 1982. (This campus ministry was built by a young couple that Kip and I converted and trained for the ministry in Charleston.) Within a couple of years, Sharon fell away. In her own words, she had grown weary and hopeless from the intense persecution by her religious family. Thankfully, God loved her enough to bring her back to Him in February 2003! Then in January 2004, her loving husband Michael was baptized! As of today, the Kirchners – because of their life experiences, their integrity and their deep love for the Bible – oversee all the administration in the SoldOut Movement Family of Churches around the world. Indeed, Michael and Sharon have become some of our dearest friends. They are truly a gift of God to Kip and me, and *"all the churches… are grateful to them."* (Romans 16:3)

From this astonishing account, *"do not be surprised"* and also do not underestimate the huge negative impact of persecution. (1 Peter 4:12) Consequently, we must strengthen those who are susceptible to persecution – Christians who are weak, sentimental and fearful – through focused Bible studies and prayers. As well, let us continue to reach out to those that have fallen. (James 5:19-20)

The third soil is where the *"seed fell among thorns, which grew up with it and choked the plant."* Jesus explains that the seed at first grows *"but as they go on their way they are choked by life's worries, riches and pleasures, and they do not mature."* This soil is contrasted with the fourth soil of *"a noble and good heart who hear the word, retain it, and by persevering produce a crop... a hundred times more."* The thorns that can choke our spiritual lives to the point that we are not bearing fruit are *"life's worries, riches and pleasures."* These thorns include financial challenges, raising children, health trials and personal disappointments, as well as the blessings of increasing salaries and higher standards of living that become all-consuming stealing our time and energy from serving God. Our lives can become so busy that our spiritual productivity gradually and so often unnoticeably is replaced with only worldly activity. Our hearts become numb or cynical or both!

Notice that fourth soil's **"noble and good hearts"** are fruitful. However, the third soil represents the hearts of people who do not **"mature"** to the point of bearing fruit and multiplying their lives by making disciples. In Hebrews, we are given a very sobering challenge about maturity, **"In fact, though by this time you ought to be teachers, you need someone to teach you the [first principles] of God's word all over again. You need milk, not solid food! Anyone who lives on milk, being still an infant, is not acquainted with the teaching about righteousness. But solid food is for the mature, who by constant use have trained themselves to distinguish good from evil."** (Hebrew 5:12-14) Maturity in this passage is equated with being a teacher of the **"first principles." "First principles"** according to Hebrews 6:1-3 are **"the foundation of repentance from acts that lead to death, and of faith in God, instructions about [baptisms], the laying on of hands, the resurrection of the dead, and eternal judgment."** So in our fellowship's vernacular, to be a teacher – to be mature – means being a Bible Talk Leader, someone that can study the Bible with another person all the way to baptism.

Maturity is vital to make it to Heaven. Often though, we are not alarmed when we see another disciple not becoming mature. After a human baby's birth, if it does not grow physically all parents become very concerned and take the baby to be in the expert care of a doctor because they are scared the baby will die. In a similar way, the Bible uses the analogy of when we are born again at baptism, that we become **"infants"** in Christ – "baby Christians." Thus, we need the "milk of first principles." This is where we all start in our Christian walk, but we must go onto maturity – mastering the first principles – and then enjoying the **"solid food"** of the deeper teachings of the Word. Maturity comes when a disciple **"who by constant use have trained themselves to distinguish good from evil."**

Since the Scriptures do not teach "once saved always saved," likewise the Bible does not support "once mature always mature." Many older Christians – in honor Kip calls them "veteran disciples" – come into our fellowship beaten up by life and have no desire to be in any form of leadership or responsibility. Showing these older disciples respect, kindness and love as we study the Bible together, helps these dear "veteran disciples" to realize that though they have been around "a long time," they are no longer mature in the faith. Through loving discipling times, brothers and sisters like Oleg and Elena Sirotkin, Matt and Helen Sullivan, and Joe and Kerry Willis have become mature again and have even gone beyond their "glory days" of the past.

Maturity includes leadership. If you are not using your time and talents in leadership, eventually you will fall away and be lost. (Matthew 25:14-30) Be sure that you are "training yourself" to have a morning quiet time, where you pray – this is how we speak to God – and read the Word – this is how God speaks to us! There are times when I get up in the morning and my mind is racing with all I have to do that day. When I give into my worries and concerns by jumping on the computer to read my emails and pay bills, I get a little "edgy" with Kip. Then he usually gently asks me, "Hey Babe, have you had your quiet time this morning?" The answer is usually "no," but there have been a few times that I did. That's when I realize that I need a longer one!

Another aspect of the secret of a noble heart is to be a light *"on a stand, so that those who come in can see the light."* A disciple must radiate *"the fruit of the Spirit… love, joy, peace, forbearance, kindness, goodness, faithfulness, gentleness, and self-control"* from a transformed life. (Galatians 5:22-23) There must be no darkness in our lives, and Jesus motivates us by saying, *"For there is nothing hidden that will not be disclosed, and nothing concealed that will not be known or brought out into the open."* If we do allow hypocrisy into our lives, God will expose it sooner or later!

To be realistic, we are still sinners. Therefore, to walk in the light is not perfection – no sin – but *"if we confess our sins, He is faithful and just and will forgive us our sins and purify us from all unrighteousness."* (1 John 1:9) James as well, encourages us to *"confess [our] sins to each other."* (James 5:16) Openness is the beginning of breaking sin's mastery over us. As we mature in Christ, it can be more difficult to confess sin, because we do not want people to look down on us as "a leader." Yet, when I remember that my sins hurt God and others especially the ones I love the most, I get open about not only my sins but also my temptations.

As one who is training younger women, I am from time to time reminded that openness breeds openness. I have found in leading discipleship groups that after I share that I have not had a visitor to church for a while, or have been fearful about Kip's and my finances, or feeling paralyzed by fears concerning challenges in my extended family, then other sisters in the group get open about similar sins and fears. Recently, after Kip made the decision that we would give $1,000 above our 20X Missions Contribution, I confessed in my "discipling group" my fears and worries and how I just needed to trust God and my husband. Immediately following several other women also shared their fears about the sacrifices for world evangelism as well. After this time of confession, we prayed. The group ended joyfully and unified. Four weeks later, the City of Angels Church blew out our Missions Contribution Goal!

SECRET TWO
-THE SECRET OF GOD'S SOVEREIGNTY -

Luke 8:22-25 – *One day Jesus said to His disciples, **"Let us go over to the other side of the lake."** So they got into a boat and set out. As they sailed, He fell asleep. A squall came down on the lake, so that the boat was being swamped, and they were in great danger.*

*The disciples went and woke Him, saying, "Master, Master, we're going to drown!" He got up and rebuked the wind and the raging waters; the storm subsided, and all was calm. **"Where is your faith?"** He asked His disciples.*

In fear and amazement they asked one another, "Who is this? He commands even the winds and the water, and they obey Him."

Before we discover this Second Secret of God's Kingdom, let's re-envision this dramatic scene of Jesus calming the storm. The text says, *"Jesus said to His disciples, 'Let's go over to the other side of the lake.' So they got into the boat and set out."* In every Renaissance painting, all by men, the artists have only placed the 12 Apostles in the boat. Yet, the text says that the *"disciples"* set out in the boat. Luke throughout his Gospel carefully distinguishes the Twelve from the *"company of disciples"* which included women. In this same chapter, in Luke 8:1-3, Luke clearly says, *"The Twelve were with Him, and also some women…"* The next portal of Jesus' ministry in this chapter is Jesus sitting with the men and women disciples that He calls family. (Luke 8:19-21) Immediately following, the text goes into the boat scene. The women must surely have been participants in this momentous event! I'm sure their screams would have added a little extra drama! Also, bookending this chapter, is Luke 9:1-2, where once more Jesus clearly distinguishes the Twelve from the other disciples by giving them miraculous powers to help people to believe when they *"proclaim the Kingdom of God."* Too often the Scriptures have been communicated from only men's perspective, even in art! In the Gospels, men and women disciples both endured the storms of life as they followed in Jesus' footsteps that cumulated at the cross.

I'm reminded of a story… Sherlock Holmes – the awesome British detective – and his assistant Dr. Watson went on a camping trip. In the middle of the night, Holmes woke Watson and said, "Watson look up and tell me what you see." Watson said, "I see millions and millions of stars." Holmes asked, "And what does that tell you?" Watson replied, "Astronomically, it tells me that there are millions of galaxies and potentially billions of planets. Theologically, it tells me that God is great and we are small and insignificant. Meteorologically, it tells me that we will have a beautiful day tomorrow. What does it tell you Holmes?" Holmes answered simply, "Somebody stole our tent!" Like Watson, most of us overlook the obvious!

The obvious of this incredible account – where Jesus calms the storm that was so violent the waves were swamping the boat – is that Jesus is Lord over all creation, both the living and the inanimate! After all, **"for by Him all things were created: things in Heaven and on earth, visible and invisible… all things were created by Him and for Him. He is before all things, and in Him all things hold together."** (Colossians 1:16-17) This is why Jesus can do miracles! From this passage, we can grasp that God is sovereign: Every event that occurs, God either makes or allows to happen. This is the God that we pray to! He really can "do something" to alter the most dire of situations… according to His will!

This secret of God's sovereignty was revealed to me through a very traumatic storm in my life in 1984. When Olivia was three years old and I was pregnant with Eric, Kip and I were first told by the doctors at Boston Children's Hospital that our son Sean, who was two at the time, had a major birth defect in his back. He had been born with five extra hemi (partially formed) vertebrates. This caused an unnatural rotation and dangerous curvature of his spine. We were informed that many children diagnosed with this condition have underdeveloped organs and die prematurely.

I did not cry at the doctor's office, I think because I was in complete denial. As Kip and I drove on Route 2 on our way back home to Lexington, I said, "Well, I think that went better than I expected." Kip looked at me in disbelief and said, "Didn't you hear what the doctor said about Sean needing an operation next year, being in a body cast for six months, probably not being able to play sports, and maybe dying early?" I immediately started uncontrollably weeping and feeling terribly overwhelmed!

When we returned home, Kip and I fell down on our knees in our bedroom and prayed for a miracle. Then Kip went downstairs to prepare for the Adult Bible Talk held in our home that Monday night. The Spirit guided him to do a study and discussion on John 9 where the man had been born blind. Kip read, **"As [Jesus] went along, He saw a man blind from birth. His disciples asked Him, 'Rabbi, who sinned, this man or his parents, that he was born blind?' 'Neither this man nor his parents sinned,' said Jesus, 'but this happened so that the works of God might be displayed in him.'"** Of course we went on to study that Jesus opened this man's eyes, which made a tremendous impact on his parents and the Jewish leaders! Few Bible Talks have been as memorable or as ministering to my soul! We shared with the whole Bible Talk about Sean's situation while asking for prayers. I was so proud of my husband that his faith was guiding me through the Scriptures to be at peace because God was at work!

The surgery was scheduled for late May 1985 at Boston Children's Hospital. This six-hour delicate procedure involved removing the discs around Sean's hemi vertebrate and the normal vertebrate above and below them. Then taking bone marrow from his hip and placing it like cement to fuse all of his lower back. The doctor communicated that he was quite pleased with the operation.

Kip spent several of the first nights in the hospital with Sean as they both watched on TV their beloved Boston Celtics in the NBA Finals! (Sometimes Kip would sneak into the hospital with McDonald's French Fries to keep Sean encouraged!) Sean proved to be a "tough cookie" because later we heard from the nurses that at night he would often break into singing his favorite Kingdom song – *Glory, Glory Hallelujah* – in his then heavy Boston accent! According to the nurses, the other three little boys in Sean's room enjoyed his singing! We had so much love, prayers and support from the Boston Church family! Meals were brought to our home; babysitting for Olivia and seven month old Eric by the college sisters allowed me to visit Sean every day; and sisters like Pat Gempel helped clean our house!

About five years later, when Sean was seven years old, we were informed by the doctor that Sean's recovery was so complete, that though he could not participate in contact sports, he was given the "green light" to participate in non-contact sports such as swimming, golf and tennis. After moving to Los Angeles in January 1990 to help with the newly planted church, I still remember Kip drawing a picture of Sean's back for him and then asking what sport that he'd like to try. After a short pause and with a big smile he said, "Tennis!" Therefore, Kip went to the Yellow Pages and made an appointment for tennis lessons. His first coach, Greg Langdon, inspired Sean to love tennis so much, that "little brother" wanted to play too! By the time Sean was 12, "big sister" joined the boys in a daily junior tennis clinic for two hours every day Monday through Friday! Subsequently, tennis became our family's sport!

Olivia, Sean and Eric were so blessed to be in this amazing junior academy. Danny Saltz, a former tennis star at UCLA and a pro who earned a world ranking of #88, oversaw it! In the next six months, Danny quickly became part of our family! Though he had a Jewish heritage, he saw something "different" in our family and started studying the Bible! On June 12, 1994, Kip baptized him into Christ! Then I remembered that Bible Talk on John 9 that our Sovereign God is at work even in our darkest times! Encouragingly, years later Danny went into the fulltime ministry!

The Spirit through Sean's disability had led us to tennis, and so the glory of God was revealed through Sean's life! Amazingly, over the next few years we baptized tennis pros: Abigail, Terry, Bounce, Andre and his wife Jaime! Two parents of junior tennis players were baptized and several ranked junior players were also baptized – including a ranked player in South Africa named Tobuku whom we met during the 1995 World Missions Leadership Conference in Johannesburg! This is the same conference where Kip spent a half-an-hour with Nelson Mandela presenting him with the HOPE Unity Award!

Since all three children were born at Mount Auburn Hospital in the Boston area, which is less than a mile from Harvard University, Kip's "impossible prayer goal" was for all three of our kids to go to Harvard! Amazingly, tennis not only allowed us to **"share our lives and the gospel with so many,"** but since all three children were nationally ranked, tennis opened the door for all three of our children to be accepted to Harvard! (1 Thessalonians 2:8) By God's grace, Olivia and Sean graduated with honors from this incredible college! Though accepted to Harvard, Eric chose to go to one of the most prominent tennis schools – Stanford University, where in time he was influential in converting the captain of the team! In Eric's senior year, he was elected captain of the Stanford Tennis Team! Truly, God is sovereign! All the storms in life are either made by God or allowed by God for His **"works to be displayed"** in our lives for His purposes!

I was reminded again about God's sovereignty in late 2006. (Sometimes we need to learn the same lesson over and over again until we "get it!") The new movement had officially just begun in Portland and both Kip and I realized that *a movement to change eternity"* must be centered in a "world city" just as the first century movement did not center in Nazareth but the largest of Jewish cities – Jerusalem! Therefore, after discussing with the Portland leaders where Kip and I should go, it seemed obvious to all of us that this city had to be in the United States. Hence, everyone quickly agreed that we needed to plant "the Jerusalem of the new movement" in either New York City or Los Angeles.

For that reason, we laid a fleece before the Lord: Whichever of these two cities that a "remnant group" would form first that would be the sign that God was guiding us there. (A remnant group in our fellowship is a gathering of disciples who "step out" of the Mainline Church of Christ or ICOC because of lukewarmness to form a church that "joins" God's new movement because they share our Biblical core convictions.) I was praying hard for New York City because I knew fewer members of what was left of the ICOC and so I felt that there would be a lot less conflict. Kip wanted to go to New York City, as he had never personally lived in New York. Well, as God would have it, just a few weeks later the remnant group of 23 came out in Los Angeles! Having had our prayers answered, we traveled to minister to the remnant group and to pray over the city on Mt. Shalom (Mt. Hollywood)! We put before the Portland Church the challenge to raise $150,000 for the planting. The Spirit planted the amazing City of Angels International Christian Church on May 7, 2007 with 42 sold-out disciples from Portland. As of today in 2016, God is using this incredible congregation as the "Jerusalem" for His new movement. He has blessed us in the City of Angels Church with an average Sunday attendance of 1,300! Yet most amazingly, in just nine years, the 42 have been multiplied by God's Spirit into almost 5,000 disciples, who are in 67 churches, in 31 nations and on all six populated continents of the world! Kip and I deeply believe that the nations will be evangelized in this generation!

I am so grateful that God led us back to Los Angeles where we had many previous relationships. God used these friendships to gather a large number of incredible "remnant disciples" into His new movement! Very early on, two dear former ministry couples placed membership: Lou Jack and Cathi Martinez and Carlos and Lucy Mejia! I will never forget my first meeting with Lucy in our apartment. She shared for two hours – often with many tears – all that Carlos and she had been through when they were asked to leave the ministry. Her faith was very weak. However, when I shared about Kip's and my similar experiences and because Lucy and I are both Latinas, I felt that God **"knit"** our souls together for something greater! (1 Samuel 18:1 KJV) Excitingly, God called Carlos and Lucy to once again serve in the fulltime ministry! They have built great churches in Washington DC, Santiago de Chile, and now in Mexico City! Today, Lucy is one of my closest friends and a very loyal sister. Truly, since God as our Father only wants the best for us, His sovereignty is so gracious!

SECRET THREE
- THE SECRET THAT ANYONE CAN CHANGE -

Luke 8:26-39 – *They sailed to the region of the Gerasenes, which is across the lake from Galilee. When Jesus stepped ashore, He was met by a demon-possessed man from the town. For a long time this man had not worn clothes or lived in a house, but had lived in the tombs.*

When he saw Jesus, he cried out and fell at His feet, shouting at the top of his voice, "What do you want with me, Jesus, Son of the Most High God? I beg you don't torture me!" For Jesus had commanded the impure spirit to come out of the man. Many times it had seized him, and though he was chained hand and foot and kept under guard, he had broken his chains and had been driven by the demon into solitary places.

*Jesus asked him, **"What is your name?"** "Legion," he replied, because many demons had gone into him. And they begged Jesus repeatedly not to order them to go into the Abyss.*

A large herd of pigs was feeding there on the hillside. The demons begged Jesus to let them go into the pigs and He gave them permission. When the demons came out of the man, they went into the pigs, and the herd rushed down the steep bank into the lake and was drowned.

When those tending the pigs saw what had happened they ran off and reported this in the town and countryside, and the people went out to see what had happened. When they came to Jesus, they found the man from whom the demons had gone out, sitting at Jesus' feet, dressed and in his right mind; and they were afraid. Those who had seen it told the people how the demon-possessed man had been cured.

Then all the people of the region of the Gerasenes asked Jesus to leave them, because they were overcome with fear. So He got into the boat and left.

*The man from whom the demons had gone out begged to go with Him, but Jesus sent him away, saying, **"Return home and tell how much God has done for you."** So the man went away and told all over town how much Jesus had done for him.*

This event takes place on the east side of the Sea of Galilee where in Jesus' day the Gentiles lived. The locals are definitely not Jews as their occupation is the keeping of pigs, which Jews are not to be in contact with or eat. The invisible, multitudinous demons who possess this man cause him to be a frightening annoyance to the people, yet these same demons recognize Jesus! Every culture and nation in that day embraced not only gods and goddesses, but also evil spirits that had great power over people. Primary to understanding these "beings" was that in every culture "lesser powers obeyed greater powers." As a result, when Jesus casts the demons out of this man, He displays the universality of His power commanding demons in the Gentile world, just as He had in the Jewish world. (Luke 4:31-36)

In this account, Jesus encounters the demoniac who runs around naked, lives among the tombs, breaks chains and in the parallel passage in Mark, we learn that **"night and day among the tombs and in the hills he would cry out and cut himself with stones."** (Mark 5:5) This man was very self-destructive. Most would not have shared with him, let alone believed that he would become a disciple!

This passage reveals the next secret – anyone can change through the power of Jesus! The Apostle John implores Christians to have deep convictions that **"the one who is in you is greater than the one who is in the world"** – Satan. (1 John 4:4) There is nothing in the world as powerful as the Holy Spirit.

Today's young women are bombarded by the media with the message that they must have the "perfect body" in order to be desirable and to have "the good life." This in turn can lead to eating disorders such as bulimia and anorexia. Make no mistake about it, demons are alive today and enter our minds through depression, criticalness, hatred, bitterness and negativity. Young women are not only cutting themselves like the demoniac of Luke 8, but they try to numb their pain through usage of excessive alcohol and illicit drugs. When even these outlets fail to bring "relief" let alone peace, often women go into a state of acedia and even become suicidal.

Today the "act of cutting" is getting more and more prevalent. In fact Bella Swan in the popular book *Twilight* engaged in this sadistic self-mutilation. Is it any wonder that young impressionable girls are drawn into this dark world by such role models? According to a recent article in *US News* by Stephanie Steinberg, "Self-injury was not studied until the late 1990's… One 2012 study of 665 youth in the journal *Pediatrics* found 7.6% of third graders and 12.7% of ninth graders self-injured. Girls are more at risk, as the study found ninth grade girls were three times more likely to self-injure compared with boys… The behavior of cutting is actually a coping strategy used to control emotions… They get sort of a rush or a high from the self-injury."[1] Sadly, even teen disciples can give into this temptation. However, in the cases with which I have been involved, once this behavior is "brought to the light" the temptation is greatly lessened and in every case with disciples, ultimately this demonic inducement is overcome.

The Center for Disease Control says that the nationwide suicide rate of girls and young women has continued to rise over the last six years. Suicide is the second leading cause of death among Americans from 10 to 24 years old after unintentional cause. Often, Christians feel helpless as well around those who are suicidal. Caution always needs to be heeded and professionals involved, but the ultimate answer lies in the power of prayer and the power of the Holy Spirit received at baptism. Jesus states, *"This kind of [self-destructive] evil spirit can only come out in prayer."* (Mark 9:29)

Interestingly, in Matthew's account of the demoniac, we learn a startling additional fact, as he writes, *"When Jesus arrived at the other side in the region of the Gadarenes, two demon-possessed men coming from the tombs met him…"* (Matthew 8:28) So Jesus "healed" two demoniacs! So is this a contradiction in the Scriptures? Absolutely not! Mark records at the end of this account, *"As Jesus was getting into the boat, the man who had been demon-possessed begged to go with Him. Jesus did not let him, but said, 'Go home to your own people and tell them how much the Lord has done for you, and how He has had mercy on you. So the man went away and began to tell in the Decapolis how much Jesus had done for him. And all the people were amazed."* (Mark 5:18-20) The "one" demoniac of which Mark and Luke record was so grateful for his healing that he preached in the Decapolis – the Ten Cities – how much Jesus had done for him. Perhaps the other was not as grateful so his response was not noteworthy. It is the same in our fellowship today; several may be baptized on the same day, but when someone becomes an evangelist – particularly given a rough background – this is the "one baptism" that is "talked about!" The one demoniac became a preacher! He was so appreciative of *"how much the Lord had done for him!"*

This account reminds me of a modern day demoniac… There was a young teenage girl who was in her own words, suicidal growing up. She would hear oppressive voices in her head that would tell her that she was no good, that she was dirty, and that everyone hated her, especially her parents. She had been molested several times by a family member, and came to believe that there was no point in living. In her anger, she would bang her head on the wall and punch herself. She satanically believed that killing herself was the only way out of her problems. She considered drowning herself, stabbing herself with a knife, and hanging herself thinking that the world would be a better place without her. The only reason that she did not give into the voices was that as the oldest child in her family, she reasoned that her siblings needed her.

Then her sister began to go to the Hilo Church of Christ that she had heard was a "cult." To check it out and rescue her, she visited but was amazed at the love and Bible teachings, and Joan (Udon) Bartholomew was baptized before her sister Jen (Ramsier)! The Holy Spirit then brought Kyle into Joan's life and they married, trained for the ministry, and now are powerfully serving the Lord fulltime as they lead the Metro Manila International Christian Church, where Joan – a Filipina – is striving to share with "her people" just **_how much the Lord has done for [her]!_** This third secret of the Kingdom will forever propel your evangelism, because anyone can change!

During all the Boston years, I had a deep conviction that "anyone can change." However, this long held belief was challenged in our second year in Los Angeles in the fall of 1991, when Kip and I decided to "help out" the fledgling AMS (Arts – Media – Sports) Ministry. This ministry was designed to reach out to the movie, television, music and media world, as well as to current and former professional athletes. In fact because of Hollywood, LA is nicknamed the "Entertainment Capital of the World." At that time, I was told that every day about 300 young people moved from around the world to "make it" in entertainment – both in front and behind the camera – which in LA is called "the business." Amusingly, we coined the phrase, "There's no business like 'soul' business!"

When we jumped into the AMS Ministry, there were about 30 disciples. During the ensuing days, other sister congregations sent into LA's AMS Ministry several professional athletes such as Cory Blackwell, who played basketball in the prestigious NBA. However, we had very few "working" actors and actresses. (In 1992, Kip and Cory initiated the Cross and Switchblade Ministry in South Central Los Angeles, but I continued to serve in the AMS Ministry bringing along our children.) One day, Kip and I were brainstorming how to baptize the amazingly talented people in the entertainment world. Then out of nowhere, Kip suggested, "Babe, why don't you become a part-time actress and at auditions and on the set reach out to actresses?" My first response was, "No way! I hate what the sins of that world have done to women! And I have absolutely no background in acting!"

A few days later, I stumbled upon a Scripture that revealed Paul's heart for the lost, *"I have made myself a slave to win as many as possible. To the Jew I became like a Jew, to win the Jew… I have become all things to all people so that by all possible means I might save some. I do this for the sake of the Gospel…"* (1 Corinthians 9:19-23) The moment that I read this passage, I knew what God was calling me to do – to venture from the secure to the insecure – in becoming a part-time actress! I had no idea where to even start, but BJ a dear sister and actress and Deke a dear brother and actor guided me. First, I had to get a set of "headshots." Then at 37 years old, I enrolled in a Commercial Actors Workshop of about 12 people. After 10 weeks of training (twice a week for three hours), representatives from various talent agencies came to see the closing night of our individual auditions. To my shock, I was blessed to be one of only two chosen! God answered my many prayers! My talent agency was Gilla Roos, headquartered in New York City and Beverly Hills.

Then to my surprise, I immediately was called for several auditions in particular for Latin women roles as a mom or as a business woman. God blessed me to appear in a few movies, do a couple "infomercials," and even be an extra several times on the then well-known TV series – *Beverly Hills 90210!* I was asked to do several print modeling pictures and even appeared in a print picture in a very special book to me by Dr. James Dobson on Christian marriage, *Love For A Lifetime*. Sadly, very early on, I was unknowingly sent on an audition for a "porn movie." Of course, I quickly left and reported this to my agent so that she would better screen my auditions. I was able to see firsthand that this world was wicked even beyond my imagination for both women and men. Another sign of the level of sin and pain in this artificial world was when Kip and I went to my Gilla Roos Christmas Party. Kip was encouraged that several people thought they had seen him in the movies, but what I remember most was how many times in our conversations people could not believe that we had been happily married for 17 years!

Now fully believing that "anyone can change" – even myself, which is at times the most difficult for us all – God allowed me to reach out to and help baptize several actresses. As well, I saw one actor baptized that I met and worked with on the movie set, *And The Band Played On*. Most memorably, a woman who I was "in competition with" at several auditions, became a good friend. I learned that she was the mistress for 17 years of a very famous singer. In time, she loved Jesus more and was baptized!

During these years in the AMS, God blessed us with an incredible facility. A Christian couple that came into the Boston Movement from the Mainline Church of Christ quite generously donated two million dollars so that the church could purchase the infamous China Club in Downtown Hollywood just a few blocks from Hollywood and Vine. The China Club had been abruptly shut down for illegal drugs, prostitution, and for breaking the fire code by having too many patrons multiple times. After totally refurbishing the inside and removing the lengthy liquor bar, Kip renamed this facility "The UpSideDown Club."

Not long after its opening, there was a live TV news story – prompted by persecution – on The UpSideDown Club. So memorably this broadcast ended very positively with the reporter saying, "Perhaps in reality the UpSideDown Club is turning lives right-side-up!" We held church services for the AMS there, as well as the monthly LA ICOC Fulltime Staff Meeting since the club had a capacity for 300 upstairs. We also hosted Actors Workshops, Open Mics, Teen Events and weddings! On the lower level, we opened a small restaurant that featured beautiful red leather booths and a sizable kitchen to have another outreach opportunity.

After two years as a part-time actress, I "retired" as the ever-increasing demands of Kip's and my family and ministry could no longer be balanced with the time that it takes for auditions and filming which could be all day and on a few occasions all night. I did learn to have a deep compassion for those who choose this profession. Indeed for years the main fountain of leadership for the Boston Movement (ICOC) was the Campus Ministry, but now a second very fruitful ministry – the AMS – provided so many to go into the fulltime ministry and part-time ministry using all of their charisma and public speaking gifts. Amazingly by 2001 when Kip and I went on sabbatical God had grown this splendid ministry to over 1,000 disciples! And to God be all the glory!

1.   Stephanie Steinburg, "What To Do If Your Child Is Cutting," US News And World Report, February 28, 2014, http://health.usnews.com/health-news/health-wellness/articles/2014/02/28/what-to-do-if-your-child-is-cutting

CHAPTER
8

Mothers, Brothers and Sisters

Luke 8:19-21 – *Now Jesus' mother and brothers came to see Him, but they were not able to get near Him because of the crowd. Someone told Him, "Your mother and brothers are standing outside, wanting to see you."* He replied, **"My mother and brothers are those who hear God's Word and put it into practice."**

The prioritizing of "spiritual family" over "physical family" is one of the most radical and controversial teachings of Christ! The church universal is our spiritual family with God as our amazing Father! In the Message Bible, this prioritization in Luke 8:21 is even more bluntly stated, **"[Jesus] replied, 'My mother and brothers are the ones who hear and do God's Word. Obedience is thicker than blood.'"** The Biblical priorities – of God, church, family and job – have been destructively compromised and satanically distorted by a seemingly "more appealing" order of: God, family, church and job. Some false prophets have even gone so far as to teach: God, family, job and then church.

In the parallel passages in the other Synoptic Gospels of Matthew and Mark, women disciples are specifically mentioned not only as **"mothers"** but as sisters as well! ***"[Jesus] replied to him, 'Who is my mother and who are my brothers?' Pointing to His disciples, He said, 'Here are my mother and my brothers. For whoever does the will of my Father in Heaven is my brother and sister and mother.'"*** (Matthew 12:48-50)

"'Who are my mother and brothers?' [Jesus] asked. Then He looked at those seated in a circle around Him and said, 'Here are my mother and my brothers! Whoever does God's will is my brother and sister and mother.'" (Mark 3:33-35)

This prioritization of "spiritual family" over "physical family" is a necessary conviction to be a sold-out disciple. This heart decision allows God to be of greater influence than any family member. Peter wholeheartedly affirms this concept and then Jesus gives an amazing promise to those who leave **"everything"** to follow Him. ***"Then Peter spoke up, 'We have left everything to follow you!' 'Truly I tell you,' Jesus replied, 'No one who has left home or brothers or sisters or mother or father or children or fields for me and the Gospel will fail to receive a hundred times as much in this present age: homes, brothers, sisters, mothers, children and fields – along with persecutions – and in the age to come eternal life.'"*** (Mark 10:28-30)

As Kyle Bartholomew, a dear brother and World Sector Leader for the Pacific Rim, has preached, "When Jesus says **'everything'** He means everything!" Notice in the above passage that jobs (fields) as well are subordinate to the Kingdom. Sadly, too many lose sight of why this prioritization is so essential. God created spiritual family – the church – to help us make it to Heaven as most physical families have different value systems than the Scriptures. In fact, Jesus promises to give – to those who are willing to leave their physical family's approval – a new and larger spiritual family, the Kingdom of God! The relationships in the Kingdom of God are some of the greatest blessings that a disciple enjoys on earth!

I feel very strongly about building family in the church, because I was raised in a tight-knit Cuban "familia" where I felt very loved and cared for! I do understand that some come into the Kingdom not having the devoted parenting that I received… and continue to receive since my parents are thankfully still alive and full of grace. Many disciples who do not have healthy family relationships – particularly with their fathers – must learn to trust God the perfect Father as well as the imperfect brothers and sisters around them.

I saw the tremendous practical value of the church being family when our first child – Olivia – was born on May 11, 1981! Though Mamá and Kip's Mom graciously each came to help us for a week, I still needed so much help after they left in learning how to be a new mother. Although there were several children in the Boston Church, Olivia was the first baby! It was so heart-warming for me to see how much all the brothers and sisters loved Olivia! The college sisters especially enjoyed carrying Olivia around the fellowship and babysitting her! They loved her like a little sister! The more mature sisters also enjoyed special moments reading to Olivia as some saw her as a daughter and others as a granddaughter! Another memorable aspect of family was when the Boston brothers and sisters pitched-in to buy a beautiful handmade, cherry wood crib crafted especially for Olivia! Of course, Sean and Eric enjoyed this "hand-me-down" crib! The crib was such a "work of art" that we later sold it for missions and received $600!

During these early years in our Boston ministry, there was a phenomenal sense of family in the church! I think this is one of the primary reasons that the congregation grew so much, **"By this everyone will know that you are my disciples, if you love one another."** (John 13:35) By 1982, the Lord had put on Kip's heart the evangelization of the nations in this generation, which included the then radical concept of planting churches rather than sending the men and women ministry leaders who we had trained into existing Mainline Churches of Christ.

Therefore, in 1982, the Spirit sent out from Boston the Chicago and London Mission Teams, and in 1983, God sent out the New York City Mission Team. By

1984, the Boston Church was multiplying as we had daily baptisms, and even more amazingly, we were 1,000 disciples meeting in the famed Boston Opera House for Sunday services!

As a result of these miracles, we received so much positive attention from the Mainline Churches of Christ and other congregations in the Crossroads Campus Ministry Movement. They witnessed the unprecedented growth and global expansion by church plantings. However, in the secular press – the *Boston Globe* and the *Harvard Crimson* – as well as in the liberal religious world, we began to receive very sharp criticisms, particularly toward our misunderstood stance on the family. But Jesus did say, ***"Do you think I came to bring peace on earth? No, I tell you, but division. From now on there will be five in one family divided against each other, three against two and two against three. They will be divided, father against son and son against father, mother against daughter and daughter against mother, mother-in-law against daughter-in-law and daughter-in-law against mother-in-law."*** (Luke 12:51-53) This stand for Christ is twisted by the world into "we did not love our physical families." However, in reality, we love our physical family even more after making Jesus Lord and being baptized! I felt this heavy criticism from the world probably too much. I wanted to encourage both friends and family alike that as Christians we loved our physical families – and all the more so – because of repenting of all bitterness and selfishness in our hearts at baptism. However, I now understand that persecution is promised and is a cross for us to carry. (John 15:20)

It was during the days of escalating persecution in 1984 that I was coming to the end of my third pregnancy in four years. Eric was due December 26th. Kip, thinking that he could make a quick, but much needed, mission trip to Sweden and Russia, set out on Thursday, November 15th arriving in Stockholm the next morning. On Sunday morning, he preached for the Stockholm Language Internship Group of 10 disciples. Shockingly, five weeks early, my water broke with Eric on Sunday morning at 6AM in Boston! I immediately prayed and called Pat for advice! Then I called Kip (no cell phones existed) a little after noon

Stockholm time, and amazingly was able to reach him! It was right after he had finished preaching!

We both felt the pressure of the incredible criticism from other churches that Kip and the Boston Church would receive if he was not in town for the birth of our third child! Well, long story short, through many prayers being answered, the brothers rushed Kip to the Stockholm airport where he secured a ticket that left Stockholm within the hour. Kip flew to London then to New York City and then he arrived at Logan Airport in Boston at 1:30AM on Monday, November 19th! A brother picked Kip up and rushed him to the hospital a little before 2AM where about 15 brothers and sisters were waiting at the hospital entrance. According to a sister, at the sight of Kip running into the hospital, everyone began clapping even some of the hospital staff! Kip made it to the fifth floor and God delivered Eric into this world at 2:19AM! Since we had not decided on a name, we named our third child Eric (a Swedish name) in honor of the Stockholm Mission Team!

Building spiritual family does not just happen! There must be preaching on this Biblical principle accompanied by a call to obedience and practical instruction. This focus must be in the congregation as a whole, but also among the leaders and in each Bible Talk. As in a physical family, competition and criticalness must be eliminated. Closeness and warm feelings should be fostered by communication that is up building and through daily encouragement. As the Bible teaches, ***"See to it, brothers and sisters, that none of you has a sinful, unbelieving heart that turns away from the living God. But encourage one another daily..."*** (Hebrews 3:12)

As mentioned in Chapter Four – THIS GENERATION – 2001 to 2003 were some of our toughest years. Persecution from the outside is bearable, but criticism within the church family is devastating. Kip and I fully realized that we were not perfect leaders and needed to listen more to those around us. As well, we failed to bring to unity some of the brothers and sisters in the ICOC World Sector Leaders Group. However, when once close brothers and sisters abandoned us, no longer accepting our leadership or even our friendship, it was crippling. Seemingly "family issues" were "used" to place Kip and me on sabbatical. However, a short time after our sabbatical began, the three real issues for many of those who opposed us came to light: 1) Our long-standing Biblical conviction that discipling is a command of God and is not optional (Matthew 28:19-20); 2) God's movement needs a central leadership with a central leader as congregational autonomy is sin (Numbers 27:12-18); and 3) The vision for the evangelization of the nations in this generation is God's will. (1 Timothy 2:3-4) Ultimately, as shared before, in April 2003 we were fired. In looking back, the "sense of family" had been lost with the ICOC's departure from these core convictions and a return to a more Mainline Church of Christ Theology. Especially in regards to church governance where each congregation no longer was under a unifying central leadership as this was dissolved and even called "unbiblical" in November 2002 at the "Long Beach Unity Meeting." Instead each ICOC congregation became autonomous – independent – as each congregation's leadership now made all their own decisions. Now it is clear: autonomous congregations foster autonomous disciples, which causes a sense of being a worldwide spiritual family to greatly diminish.

In July 2003, Kip and I drove out of our beloved Los Angeles to begin our new ministry in Portland, Oregon. During the drive, we were in tears reminiscing about all the miracles over the last almost 13 years in LA. We felt totally alone, but this caused us to draw closer to God and each other. We knew that in Portland that we had to rebuild this "sense of family" in this hurting congregation whose membership had plunged in 2003 from 300 members to just 25 members, who were still committed to Midweek Services. We met in small groups with many of the members who had drifted away, as well as individually to listen to their perspectives. So on August 13, 2003, we had a Midweek Service that we called "The Evening of Atonement." At this inspiring session, Kip instructed everyone who attended that they could only come to the front of the auditorium and share their own shortcomings and sins. Tony Untalan volunteered to start. He apologized from his heart in tears for his anger and bitterness toward many in the church. This apology moved all of us to cry! Then Jeremy Ciaramella followed with the same **"broken and contrite heart."** (Psalm 51:17) We were there until 10PM as the members of the Portland Church forgave each other and committed to being a merciful family. The membership quickly "jumped" to around 100 as this was such a powerful and healing time for us as a congregation! This collective repentance brought **"times of refreshing"** as God once again began to bless the Portland Church with baptisms! (Acts 3:19)

From the beginning, we focused on building family as one of our main themes. One sister suggested that we needed a special way "to welcome" new members to the family. Kip had been reading Exodus and remembered that there were **"women who served at the entrance to the Tent of Meeting."** (Exodus 38:8) So we decided that at our church services, we would have the "Sisters of Encouragement" introduce and warmly welcome the new members with a $15 Starbucks Gift Card! Then we would sing as a church to the new members, *We Love You With The Love Of The Lord!* We would then take a short break to give them big hugs!

Sadly, in our former fellowship as they returned to "Mainline Theology," the women were "pushed out" of almost all leadership meetings – giving little or no input into decisions. Though I do not believe that a woman should lead the church as an Evangelist, I do believe that a strong women's presence in the church fosters nurturing and gentleness that are vital for a healthy church! Paul in 1 Thessalonians shares the "feminine qualities" that Silas, Timothy and he displayed in this very successful planting: **"Just as a nursing mother cares for her children, so we cared for you because we loved you so much."** (1 Thessalonians 2:7-8)

This sense of family carried over to our welcoming and hosting disciples who flew into visit the Portland Church! As mentioned before, more and more disciples moved to Portland from all over the United States to be revived and get convictions that discipling is a command of God that will help us get to Heaven! Therefore, sacrificial disciples would drive to the Portland Airport to affectionately greet these hurting disciples with this same song of love – *We Love You With The Love Of The Lord!* This is now a custom throughout the SoldOut Movement

Churches to sing at the airport to disciples coming in from other places. I will never forget when I was greeted by about 20 disciples with this welcome at the Santiago de Chile Airport in 2010, as I heard this song for the first time in my heart language of Spanish! It made me well up with tears of joy in seeing my *"familia!"*

On a personal level, I needed this sense of family too! Two couples of the 25 original members of the Portland Church – Tony and Therese Untalan and Nick and Denise Bordieri – quickly became true brothers and sisters to Kip and me! Therese was converted on the island of Guam in 1997 and moved to Portland in 1999. I was drawn to her "island warmth," to her great love for the Bible, and to her humility even though she was Miss Guam in 1985! Denise was influenced by a friend in the Philippines to become a Christian in Portland in 2001. She was an easy sister for me to become close to because of her serving heart as she hosted in her home most of the early leadership meetings. As well, during our Portland days, Denise often would go out of her way to give me rides for studies and appointments.

Our bond with the Untalans was also strengthened through their daughters – Coleen and Tesoni. They quickly became like daughters to us! In fact in time, Tony and Therese asked us to become the girls' legal guardians if anything ever happened to the two of them. We were greatly honored by this request and level of trust. In addition, Kip presided at Coleen and Ricky's wedding! Tesoni has already asked Kip to officiate her wedding someday too! The Bordieris' daughters – Sonrisa and Makaela – are likewise very special to us, as the entire Bordieri family has celebrated "Noche Buena" (Christmas Eve) every year with our family since 2003! Today, the Bordieris and Untalans serve as Shepherding Couples not only for us and the City of Angels Church, but also for the entire SoldOut Movement!

I am so blessed to have a mother and mother-in-law who have mastered the art of creating a warm and loving home. They remind me of Proverbs 11:16, ***"A kind-hearted woman gains honor."*** I truly honor Mamá and Kip's mom – Kim! I also appreciate Kip's dad – "Admiral Tom McKean" – as he is one of the most impressive men that I have known. He is very respectful towards women and so caring about the less fortunate of the world. Since our wedding, I call Kip's parents: "Dad" and "Mom"! Of course, my Papá is a very remarkable gentleman, a compassionate father and a generous soul. At 89 years old, he remains a hero for me!

Another family member who I adored because of her encouragement to my spiritual life is my Tía Margarita. Though very excitable, she was always so sweet and kind. Her daughter – my first cousin – Maruchi is my age and is just as enthusiastic about life as her mom! Of course, my older sister Carmen had a very profound impact on my life. She not only led me to Christ, but also remains an upward call as she and her husband served gallantly on the mission fields of Central and South America!

Jesus was not the only one to build family masterfully, but also Paul. In Romans 16, he commended **"our sister Phoebe"** to the Rome Church. He goes on to lift up other women that were courageous and hardworking: Priscilla, Mary, Junia, Tryphena, Tryphosa, his **"dear friend Persis,"** and Nereus' sister. Yet most endearingly, Paul wrote, **"Greet Rufus, chosen in the Lord, and his mother, who has been a mother to me, too."** (Romans 16:13) Inspiringly, Rufus' mom was married to Simon of Cyrene – the man who carried Jesus' cross! (Mark 15:21) Though it is a fact that every true Christian is our brother or sister in Christ, the sense of being family takes extraordinary efforts and time! It is often overlooked that Paul "made" individuals in God's church his close spiritual family! Every Christian should strive to imitate his example. So if you are lonely in the church, realize that you must initiate relationships to "make family."

The Scriptures are true that God blesses us with so much more spiritual family! Since I left Cuba at such a young age, I was never really close to my physical grandmothers, but in Christ, Irene Gurganus was my "spiritual Abuela" (Grandmother)! The Gurganuses moved to Boston in their late 60's to train and serve in the Boston Church as they had spent years in the Mainline Church of Christ building Missions Programs at both Harding and Abilene Universities. Then after two years, at almost 70 years old, Irene accompanied her husband George to go back to the challenging mission field of Tokyo, Japan. I'll never forget her last words to me shortly before her death, "If Pope (George) would still be living, he'd be side-by-side with Kip in the new movement!"

Of course, Pat Gempel is still my spiritual mom and has been there for my family and me for 38 years – since 1979! Often when I am in tough situations, I still ask myself, "What would Pat do?" Pat taught me so much about the importance of building spiritual family.

God has refreshed my heart through all the spiritual sisters He has given me in His new movement. So dear to my heart but by no means a complete list are: Therese Untalan, Denise Bordieri, Helen Sullivan, Sharon Kirchner, Kerry Willis, Sonja Chloupek, Sonia Gonzalez, Connie Underhill, Jeanne McGee, Patricia Feumba, Prisca Scheidecker, Burgandie Onekea, Megan Mathews, Maria Jose Tria, Pam Boea, Maria Hart, Susan Bond and Lana Douglas – one of the original "30 would-be disciples" of Boston!

I really love being a Mom! Therefore, my spiritual daughters through all the years are as Jesus said, ***"A hundred times as much!"*** God has given me so many encouraging relationships with spiritual daughters: Lianne Kernan, Patrique Smellie, Michele Williamson, Lynda Moreno, Lucy Mejia, Joan Bartholomew, Elena Sirotkina, Jee Blackwell, Cathi Martinez, Shay Sears, Anu Arneson, Kacie Jimenez, Cyndee Ochs, Brandyn Speckman, Debs Rajan, Nathalie Fetelika, Sarah Dimitry, Coleen Challinor, Tesoni Untalan, Kelly Bartholomew, Alejandra Anuch, Kerri-Sue Adams, Tracy Harding, Amy Ciaramella, Angelica Grima, Yelena Astanina, Gina dela Pena, Anna Malnegro, Maika Carbonell, Melina Hairston, Cecy Frazier, Brittany Underhill, Courtney Parlour, Patricia Velasco, Rachel McGee, Julia Soboleva, Erica Kim, Donna Lamb – who died in the Lord – and so very dear is Rebecca Rico as she labors with Kip and me on the Good News Emails during those oh so long Mondays and this book!

I love being an "Abuela" too! My spiritual granddaughters include Avrie Blackwell, Sonrisa and Makaela Bordieri, Sofia and Lidia Sirotkina, Naomi Smellie, Melissa and Amanda Sullivan, Shefali and Isheeta Rajan, Bella Moreno, Jash and

Jorge Malnegro, Bree Bartholomew, Mia Williamson, Ann Cathrine Arneson, Helena and Odelia Feumba, Christine Martinez, Sarah Ochs, Priscilla and Daniela Velasco, as well as all the ICCM sisters like Daniela Woody, Cassidy Olmos, Margie Hamula, Krista Ochieng, Debbie Limon, Krystal Legarda, Kristtina Javierre, Joy George, Sonia Green, Karen Maciel, Carol Postigo, Tatty Bonilla and several other women interns in our family of churches!

Family is paramount to being God's church. With that in mind, Kip and I wrestled with what to do at our very first World Sector Leaders Meeting for the new movement on Wednesday, August 6, 2014. At that time, Kip read from 1 Corinthians 11 and we were reminded that the unleavened bread represents the unified body of Christ; the red juice represents the crimson blood of Christ who paid the ultimate price for our salvation. All the new World Sector Leaders were seated in a circle and as each one took the bread, each would hold it before the group and say, "We are family." Then each one would take the one cup of grape juice, and hold it before the group and pledge, "To the end." This has now become the heart of God's new SoldOut Movement, "We are family… to the end."

Jesus was all about family. This was on His heart even during the excruciating pain suffered on the cross. ***"When Jesus saw His mother there, and the disciple whom He loved (the Apostle John) standing nearby, He said to her, 'Woman, here is your son,' and to the disciple, 'Here is your mother.' From that time on, this disciple took her into his home."*** (John 19:26-27) To the very end, Jesus loved His physical family.

This Heavenly conviction of the prioritization of "spiritual family over physical family" had a tremendous impact on Jesus' mother and brothers! After the resurrection, we find Jesus' mother and brothers among the faithful ***"hundred and twenty"*** of Acts 1:14-15 that formed the foundation of the early church! Amazingly by applying this simple but challenging principle, Jesus' persecuting mother and brothers, who at one time thought He was ***"out of His mind,"*** became His spiritual family! (Mark 3:21) If we imitate Jesus, we too will see family members added to God's Kingdom!

CHAPTER
9

Sick and Dying

Luke 8:40-48 – *Now when Jesus returned, a crowd welcomed Him, for they were all expecting Him. Then a man named Jairus, a synagogue leader, came and fell at Jesus' feet, pleading with Him to come to his house because his only daughter, a girl of about 12, was dying. As Jesus was on His way, the crowds almost crushed Him. And a woman was there who had been subject to bleeding for 12 years, but no one could heal her. She came up behind Him and touched the edge of His cloak, and immediately her bleeding stopped.*

"Who touched me?" Jesus asked. When they all denied it, Peter said, "Master, the people are crowding and pressing against you." But Jesus said, "Someone touched me; I know that power has gone out from me." Then the woman, seeing that she could not go unnoticed, came trembling and fell at His feet. In the

presence of all the people, she told why she had touched
Him and how she had been instantly healed. Then He
*said to her, "**Daughter, your faith has healed you. Go in***
peace."

In this last portion of the Women's Elevation Section, Luke again employs the literary device of "balance." The balance in this passage is the healing of the 12 year old girl and the healing of the older woman who had been bleeding for 12 years. So the message is simply that Jesus came to heal (save) "the young" and "the old" – which encompasses the entire world! This Gospel to the Gentiles — the Book of Luke — repeatedly radiates the message spoken by Simeon in the temple courts as he affectionately held the baby Jesus in his arms, *"For my eyes have seen your salvation, which you have prepared in the sight of all nations: A light for revelation to the Gentiles, and the glory of your people Israel."* (Luke 2:30-32) In addition to this, the number 12 is significant in Scripture as it is symbolic of God's people – the 12 Israelite Tribes of Physical Israel and the 12 Apostles of Spiritual Israel, the church. Once again, God is communicating to us that He is concerned with the well-being of "the young" and "the old," and His desire is that they both be healed, thus becoming His spiritual family!

Jesus' message and miracles were becoming well known, so much so that He had become quite a celebrity! Different than worldly celebrities or even most religious ones of our day, when Jesus was in a crowd of people not one person was ever ignored. Peter could not believe that Jesus felt the touch of an individual in this pressing mob. To add to the drama, the Jews of that day understood that because of this woman's bleeding she was unclean and therefore an outcast according to Leviticus 15:25-27. These purity laws required her to be quarantined; *"Anyone who touches [a woman with a discharge of blood] will be unclean."*

Mark's Gospel is more detailed and adds, *"She had suffered a great deal under the care of many doctors and had spent all she had, yet instead of getting better she grew worse.*" Many commentators have suggested that Luke's omission of this information was that he was a doctor and did not want to give his profession any "bad press!" That said, this information tells us that not only was this woman's bleeding a 12-year-long ordeal, but that her condition was seemingly incurable.

Most, in her situation, would be hopeless and lay paralyzed at home. Yet this courageous woman of faith, in her desperation left the isolation imposed on her and in her weakened physical condition, braved the crowds risking the consequences of breaking the Law. After Jesus said, *"Someone touched me! [Then] in the presence of all the people,"* she volunteered that she was the one who had *"touched Him and had been instantly healed."* Jesus – perhaps with a smile – expressed His warmth and said, *"Daughter, you took a risk trusting me, and now you're healed and whole. Live well, live blessed!"* (Luke 8:48 MSG) So Jesus rewarded and commended her phenomenal faith! Of note, Jesus did not become unclean when she touched the hem of His garment, because she was immediately healed… and therefore, ceremonially clean!

In this passage, the Greek word translated *"healed"* is *"sozo."* Interestingly, according to Thayer's Greek Lexicon, *"sozo"* is used 19 times throughout the Book of Luke and 110 times in the New Testament. It means "to save" a suffering one from disease or "to save" and rescue one in danger of destruction. Captivatingly, this same word is used in Acts 2:21, *"And everyone who calls on the name of the Lord will be saved (sozo)!"* And in Acts 4:12, *"Salvation is found in no one else, for there is no other name under Heaven given to mankind by which we must be saved (sozo)!"* In the New Testament *"sozo"* conveys the deeper meaning of not just a physical healing, but also spiritual healing. Salvation is so much more than just having all our sins forgiven; it is the "healing" of our hearts, souls and minds!

In the City of Angels Church, our theme for 2014 was "The Year of Prayer." In early April of that year, my personal physician told me that my calcium had risen significantly from my last check up in December 2012 and that I had lost weight.

She was concerned and wanted to do more blood tests. This prompted me to share with her that I had been feeling tired and dizzy quite often for the past few months. I had rationalized that I was just getting older as I was coming up in September on my 59th birthday.

The next week, I came in with Kip to hear the test results. She very calmly said that my calcium in December 2012 was 10.7 – a little high as the average person is around 10.0. Then she added that now my calcium was a very concerning 11.2. Finally, she said that the blood test showed a cancer marker of 0.5. (A cancer marker is the presence of a protein given off by cancer cells or a protein given off by white blood cells in fighting cancer.) My doctor urgently expressed that I needed an appointment that day to see an oncologist who specialized in multiple myeloma (bone cancer). This was so surreal and I reminded Kip that Tía Margarita had died of this same cancer. We prayed as we pulled off to the side of the road for God to work a miracle.

When Kip and I first saw the oncologist a few days later, he began by saying, "Upon the diagnosis of bone cancer, patients usually live three months to three years, but more and more are living with improved treatment to five years. This particular cancer always responds to chemotherapy but always returns. In effect, it is incurable." Therefore, several more tests were scheduled: urine tests, blood tests, a bone marrow biopsy, and a complete body bone scan.

We shared our distressing news with our children and our closest brothers and sisters. When I phoned my parents, my Papá cried and said, "Mamá and I will be praying for a miracle." Mamá had breast cancer twenty years before and advised me to research intensely this cancer and go after getting my body strong.

There were two guiding Scriptures for me. The first Psalm 34:17, **"The righteous cry out, and the Lord hears them; He delivers them from all their troubles."** This inspirational Scripture brought to mind Hezekiah's prayer to God to heal him after he was told by Isaiah that he would die from his horrendous boil. (Isaiah 38:1-5) God graciously answered Hezekiah's prayer and granted him 15 more years of life. The second guiding Scripture taught, **"Trust in the Lord**

with all your heart and lean not on your own understanding; in all your ways submit to Him and He will make your paths straight… This will bring health to your body and nourishment to your bones." (Proverbs 3:5-8) I was not afraid to die because I do believe in Heaven as a much better place, but I felt that I had not completed my life's purpose for God. (Acts 13:36) So I begged the Lord in tears daily for 20 more years of life so that I could see all of my family in Christ and the nations of the world evangelized!

After researching multiple myeloma, Kip and I decided that we would start "juicing" in the morning and night. We did this as a form of fasting and also to strengthen my immune system. We continued for almost two months. I know many of our close friends and family were praying. The weekend after Mother's Day, we travelled to San Francisco to help our sister church with leadership transitions. On our return to LA on Monday morning at the San Francisco Airport, I felt absolutely terrible – very weak and extremely dizzy! So much so that while standing in line to board, I just had to sit down on the ground! Kip was very alarmed and asked if he needed to call a doctor or an ambulance. As I plopped down on the floor, I closed my eyes. I begged God to help me and give me enough strength to fly home and to count the cost with Sofia Sirotkina that night. Very amazingly, about ten minutes later, Kip helped me up to board the plane and I felt much better! I counted the cost with Sofia that night and she was baptized the next day at our City of Angels Church Staff Meeting! I sensed something had changed!

Kip and I returned to my oncologist on June 11th. The doctor came in with a smile on his face and said, "I have amazing news for you guys!" He mumbled as if speaking to himself, "Maybe it was all a mistake, but it can't be!" Then he said more coherently, "It must be a miracle as I know you both are ministers and you pray! Elena, your calcium is 9.8 and there are no cancer markers to be found! In all of my years of practicing medicine, I have never seen anything like this!" Of course, I was euphoric and began to thank God! Then, the doctor added to Kip's dismay, "But you still have activity in your bone marrow at a microscopic level… but many people do. So please come back in November and let's recheck everything."

We were so fired-up that we immediately called our families and shared with all our friends this great news! Again, Papá cried! He said, "This is a miracle!" Well, in November after more tests, we returned once again to the oncologist. This time he said, "You're all clear! Elena don't take this wrong, but I never want to see you again!" I'm praying that he will not under these circumstances!

I learned to trust God on a deeper level instead of worrying, which for years has been one of my core sins. I became surrendered and in complete submission to whatever His will is for my life. I discovered at a higher level the power of prayer and fasting. Both are needed! I came to understand that my Father in Heaven is even more gracious than I had ever imagined, and He wants to answer our prayers!

I learned to treasure every day and make it count for God and His Kingdom! My sense of joy in serving God was so reinvigorated! I was also very sobered that God mercifully gave me more time! Another powerful lesson that God showed me through my Mamá's advice, when I first found out that I had cancer, was, "Elena you must strengthen your body as much as possible." God has wonderfully made our bodies very resilient, yet we need to take care of our physical bodies. A vital principle is taught in 1 Corinthians 6:19-20, **"Do you not know that your bodies are temples of the Holy Spirit, who is in you, whom you have received from God? You are not your own; you were bought at a price. Therefore honor God with your bodies."** According to the Scriptures, our bodies are the **"temples of the Holy Spirit!"**

During the days of my cancer, I had to learn "to listen" to my body when I was extremely weak and dizzy. It was time to rest and pray! A healthy amount of sleep is a way that God heals our bodies. According to Dr. P. Murali Doraiswamy, a brain researcher at Duke University, "Sleeping less than seven or eight hours a night has been linked to cognitive decline, memory loss and possibly even Alzheimer's new research shows… Chemicals secreted during the deeper stages of sleep are crucial for repairing the body – including the brain."[1] All of us are unique; we must pray for wisdom and figure out what will make our bodies healthy – proper diet, adequate sleep, exercise and a "grateful to God" mental attitude!

As far as sleep goes, Psalm 127:2 clearly says, **"In vain you rise early and stay up late, toiling for food to eat – for He grants sleep to those He loves."** Having restful sleep is something marvelous that God grants us! Yet many Americans are hard-driving, stressed and consumed with all kinds of worries. Doctors now warn against this dangerous type of life-style. (Matthew6:25-34) I did rest more when I was battling cancer as God granted me sleep.

As far as my diet, I deepened my convictions to take care of the temple that God gave me. There's a lot of amazing research online about nutrition which makes a vital difference in our health. Huge concerns for me are the eating disorders such as anorexia and bulimia that are plaguing many young women and even costing some of them their lives. For me, the seriousness of eating disorders first came to light in 1983 with the death of Karen Carpenter, one of Kip's and my favorite singers. (We used one of the popular Carpenter songs in our wedding – *We've Only Just Begun*.) Quite shockingly, Karen Carpenter died from anorexia complications at just 32 years old.

Eating disorders have been dramatically increasing at an alarming rate. In the church, we need to foster and teach about healthy life-styles. It is "spiritual" to take care of your body, of course without being obsessive. I do believe the "juicing" that Kip and I did as well as eating healthier was another big part of God healing me, though I believe prayers and God's mercy were the ultimate keys in my cancer being taken away by God! Another concern that the medical world has raised is obesity and all the intense health challenges that come along with this epidemic. As Christians we must honor God through "how much or how little we eat" and "what we eat" to make sure that it is beneficial for our bodies – **"the temples of the Holy Spirit!"**

Another area for disciples to work on is our "mental attitude" and how it affects our emotions, our health and thus our spiritual well-being. The medical community has only recently validated several principles that have been in the

Bible for thousands of years. In Proverbs 17:22, *"A cheerful heart is good medicine, but a crushed spirit dries up the bones."* Also, in Proverbs 16:24, *"Gracious words are a honeycomb, sweet to the soul and healing to the bones."* During the days of my cancer, there were many times when I had to set my mind and pray to trust God with my health, especially when I was not feeling well at all. Even now, I strive daily in my prayers to not give into fears about my future, but instead to "graciously" serve God's people, being determined to courageously partner with my amazing husband Kip to evangelize the nations. Heavy on my heart is the desire to help our precious grandchildren grow up in this so-often-cruel world with spiritual values and understanding God's unconditional love.

Another lesson that both Kip and I learned was "to enjoy and celebrate the victories" along the way! In 1986 when we first travelled to Argentina, a dear brother told us about Iguazu Falls. We learned that as glorious as Niagara Falls was in America and Canada, Iguazu – located between Brazil and Argentina – was even more so! Three main falls compose Niagara Falls, but Iguazu has 275 falls and they are twice as high as Niagara! For years and years, we talked about visiting these fabled falls, but we never found the time (or money) as there were always "more urgent" things to do!

Then in 2014 after the November "all clear" doctor's report, we decided that during our next trip to South America we would finally celebrate our 38th Wedding Anniversary and (a bit belatedly) Kip's 60th birthday, as he did not want to really celebrate in May 2014 due to my cancer. Therefore, since we were scheduled to preach in Sao Paulo, Brazil, we spent our own money to buy two round-trip tickets to Iguazu from Sao Paulo after our efforts there in February 2015. We used points to pay for our hotel stay and spent three of the most restful and glorious days celebrating our anniversary and Kip's birthday in God's modern day "Garden of Eden!" Yes, by taking the time (and money) to celebrate, we returned home closer to each other, as well as refreshed and ready to work hard for the Lord! For too long and in too many instances, I replaced the important with the urgent.

My last observation about this wonderful account in Luke 8:43-48 where the woman touches Jesus' cloak, is that Jesus shares, *"I know that power has gone out from me."* The Holy Spirit of God gives us supernatural spiritual, emotional and physical power and strength. Paul encourages all Christians to grasp the power that the Holy Spirit gives to them, *"I pray that the eyes of your heart may be enlightened in order that you may know... His incomparably great power for us who believe. That power is the same as the mighty strength He exerted when He raised Christ from the dead..."* (Ephesians 1:18-20) That said, when a disciple reaches out and studies the Bible with people, our efforts to heal their lives and save their souls can be particularly exhausting. But this is what it takes! Paul writes about *"great endurance... hard work and sleepless nights... [and being sustained by] the power of God"* as necessary to bring salvation to others. (2 Corinthians 6:5-7) This does not contradict but complements being wise about your schedule, health and taking care of God's temple because we can rely on God's power!

At the end of his life, Paul adds, *"For I am already being poured out like a drink offering, and the time for my departure is near. I have fought the good fight, I have finished the race, I have kept the faith. Now there is in store for me the crown of righteousness, which the Lord... will award to me... [and] to all who have longed for His appearing."* (2 Timothy 4:6-8) Paul saw his entire Christian life as being *"poured out"* for the sake of others' salvation. He uses the vision of a *"drink offering"* to help us understand his heart. In Numbers 28 – 29, the *"drink offering"* is addressed 27 times. In essence, red wine was poured over the animal sacrifice and since this offering was made over a fire, it released *"an aroma pleasing to the Lord."* (Numbers 28:8) Paul wanted us to envision his red blood – his life – as one that was *"poured out"* over the sacrifice of the "Lamb of God" and produced an aroma that is *"pleasing to the Lord."* This too is my heart for my life to be *"poured out"* till nothing is left but my entrance to Heaven with all whom I have influenced for Christ!

1.   Gabrielle de Groot Redford, "Why Sleep Is Precious," AARP, December 2014, Page 23

CHAPTER
10

Get Up!

Luke 8:49-56 – *While Jesus was still speaking, someone came from the house of Jairus, the synagogue leader. "Your daughter is dead," he said. "Don't bother the teacher anymore." Hearing this, Jesus said to Jairus,* **"Don't be afraid; just believe, and she will be healed."**

When He arrived at the house of Jairus, He did not let anyone go in with Him except Peter, John and James, and the child's father and mother. Meanwhile, all the people were wailing and mourning for her. **"Stop wailing,"** *Jesus said.* **"She's not dead but asleep."**

They laughed at Him, knowing that she was dead. But He took her by the hand and said, **"My child, get up!"** *Her spirit returned, and at once she stood up. Then Jesus told them to give her something to eat. Her parents were astonished, but He ordered them not to tell anyone what had happened.*

The Women's Elevation Section – Luke 7:11 to Luke 8:56 – incorporates the literary device of "balance" as it begins with the resurrection of the powerless widow's only son and concludes with the resurrection of the powerful synagogue ruler's only daughter. So the encrypted message of resurrection for all mankind is encompassed in the "male (son) / female (daughter)" and the "powerless / powerful" motifs.

Since Jairus' name is in the Scriptures, we can surmise that he became a disciple and a leader in the early church. Most likely Jairus was a prosperous man as he was the ruler of the synagogue. "Ruler" is the translation of the Greek word "archon" in verse 41. In verse 49, Jairus is called *"archisunagogou"* – synagogue ruler. His responsibilities for this esteemed role are to oversee synagogue worship by selecting those who lead prayer, read Scripture, and teach in the worship service. Though never mentioned in Scripture as a command of God, the "synagogue system" emerged in Israel after the Jews returned from Babylon to Israel, thus having its gestation during the captivity. Well known is that Jesus taught in the synagogues, thus approving of the synagogue concept. In essence, the purpose of this system, according to Ed Vasicek, was "for the Jews to have a system to indoctrinate their people and to hold one another accountable."[1]

Most commentators assume this double miracle account of the healing of the bleeding woman and the raising of the dead girl is centered in Capernaum – Jesus' home – as this section of Scripture begins, ***"Now when Jesus returned…"*** (Luke 8:40) The crowd on the beach ***"welcomed [Jesus] for they were all expecting Him"*** to return from the region of the Gerasenes by boat. Most likely in the crowd was Jairus, as he desperately hoped that Jesus would arrive in time to heal his ***"only daughter."***

This passage becomes all the more endearing when we understand that the phrase ***"only daughter"*** ("monogenes" in Greek) most likely carries a sense of deep affection. She was "Daddy's little girl." This belief is reinforced in Mark's Gospel as Jairus is recorded as saying, ***"My little girl is dying."*** (Mark 5:23)

As soon as Jesus got out of the boat, the crowd pressed against Him. Yet, the crowd soon parted in deference to Jairus, who as the synagogue ruler was one of the most respected men in the city. Jairus also was most likely the one who invited Jesus to speak in "his" synagogue which is the one in Capernaum. (Luke 4:31) This moving scene has two men who know each other, yet when Jairus reaches Jesus *"he fell at Jesus' feet."* The Greek word that Luke uses here is "pison", which means to fall down, to throw oneself to the ground as a sign of coming into the presence of a much higher ranking or divine person. Viewed in this paradoxical scene is the well-dressed synagogue ruler falling humbly before the plainly dressed Jesus!

Seemingly on His way to Jairus' home, Jesus was slowed down by the enthusiastic crowd of well-wishers, and then even stopped to converse with the woman who was healed of the flow of blood. It is at this euphoric moment that the terrible news came to Jairus, *"Your daughter is dead... Don't bother the Teacher anymore."* Jesus overhears this tragic news. Perhaps with His hand on Jairus' shoulder, He said to Jairus, *"Don't be afraid; just believe, and she will be healed."* Jairus must have believed, because he takes Jesus to his house!

Upon arriving at Jairus' home, Jesus' three closest disciples – Peter, John and James – and the girl's parents come into the house with Jesus. Jesus saw the little girl, but continued to hear what must have been annoying wailing. So from inside the house, Jesus rebuked the mourners, *"Stop wailing! She is not dead but asleep."* So different from Jairus' reverent faith, the mourners just laughed at Jesus! They believed the girl would be buried by nightfall. These "mourners" cried one moment and the next they laughed at Jesus! People can be so fickle and insincere.

Then, Jesus compassionately took the girl's hand and softly said, *"My child, get up!"* Luke records, *"Her spirit returned, and at once she stood up!"* Evidently, the girl did not lie there trying to "collect her strength." The parents were in awe and stunned! I think Jesus with a pleased smile said to the parents, *"Give her something to eat."* If indeed Jesus and Jairus were more than mere acquaintances in this small community, Jesus would have known this young woman. In fact, there is that sense that He knew her as Jesus addresses her as **"My child."**

Of no small importance, Luke records that the girl is to be served food. After all, if one remains sick and dying, one usually does not have a desire to eat. Secondly, this indicates that the girl had been raised not just in "spirit" but as "flesh and blood" with all her human needs and desires.

In the past, I have asked the question, "Why did Jesus command the parents not to tell anyone?" First of all, when news of Jesus' miracles did "get out," it restricted His movements. This is precisely what happened when Jesus healed the leper, **"Jesus sent him away at once with a strong warning: 'See that you don't tell this to anyone...' Instead he went out and began to talk freely, spreading the news. As a result, Jesus could no longer enter a town openly but stayed outside in lonely places. Yet the people still came to Him from everywhere."** (Mark 1:43-45)

Another reason that Jesus told Jairus and his wife to be silent about this amazing miracle was that He did not want to be prematurely hailed as the Messiah. He still had so much to teach! Indeed, when the Jewish leaders saw how everyone went after Him as the Messiah, that's when they made a set plan to kill Jesus. (John 11:53) Immediately following, it is recorded, **"Jesus no longer moved about publically."** (John 11:54)

The key verse for me in this exciting passage is, **"My child, get up!"** Jesus knows each of us as He knew this young woman. When our hand is in His hand, Jesus gives us not only the strength but the command to **"get up"** – to *ELEVATE!*

As a disciple for almost 43 years, I have fallen in my faith on not a few occasions. There is pain in all of our lives. The first of two Scriptures that has inspired me not to linger in pain and self-pity is Proverbs 24:16, **"For though a righteous [woman] falls seven times, [she] rises again, but the wicked are brought down by calamity."** The other motivational passage is found in Micah 7:7-8, **"But as for me, I watch in hope for the Lord, I wait for God my Savior; my God will hear me... Though I have fallen, I will rise. Though I sit in darkness, the Lord will be my light."**

I write this book to encourage all of the women that read it, and also as a humble appeal to my awesome brothers who shoulder the final decisions for God's churches. So dear brothers, please consider 1 Chronicles 12:32 in the light of women in today's world. I pray that you will be *"men... who understood the times and knew what Israel [the church] should do."* I beg you that to win as many souls as possible, to win as many women as possible, that like Jesus you will *ELEVATE* the view and value of women's leadership in your congregation.

My husband Kip has endured much criticism for striving to have women participate in church services – not with any authority over men – but to have opportunities to share their hearts and lives especially during communion or contribution. I appreciate that Kip recognizes how important it is for sisters to serve not only as "Kids Kingdom Teachers," but also as ushers and "Sisters of Encouragement" who warmly and graciously welcome those who place membership. Also, Kip has encouraged brothers to allow sisters more opportunities to assist in congregational singing and from time to time, perform a solo song expressing their love for God as did Mary the mother of Jesus (Luke 1:46-55), Hannah the mother of Samuel (1 Samuel 2:1-10), and Miriam the sister of Moses (Exodus 15:20-21).

Also, Kip has taught that women baptizing other women into Christ is "not prohibited" in the Scriptures. He persuasively reasoned with the other brothers in the early 1990's that Matthew 28:19-20 – the Great Commission – fully applies to men and women. Jesus commands, *"Go and make disciples of all nations, baptizing them in the name of the Father and the Son and the Holy Spirit, and teaching them to obey everything I have commanded you. And surely I am with you always to the very end of the age."*

Kip dissected this Scripture and gently taught his fellow preachers that we want our sisters to *"Go"* – in other words to share their faith. We desire our dear sisters to *"make disciples"* – to study the Bible with other women. We absolutely need our sisters to go to *"all nations"* – to be on mission teams. And after baptism, we expect our sisters to disciple the newly baptized women *"to obey*

everything [that Jesus] commanded." So we are missing but one aspect of the Great Commission to be asked of our sisters – **"baptizing!"** For a woman to baptize another woman brings great joy and does not violate 1 Timothy 2:12, **"I do not permit a woman to teach or to assume authority over a man."**

In addition, I humbly beg my dear brothers to *ELEVATE* "the woman's voice" in influencing the affairs of the church. Just as a wife "has a voice" in the raising of her and her husband's children, so I appreciate Kip's sensitivity to have sisters involved in leadership decisions, submissively giving their heartfelt input. This godly pattern began in our ministry back in the early days of Boston in the 1980's. Often, I would overhear Kip talk with the brother leaders during their meetings in the living-room, while I was in another part of the house. Then privately I would share my heart with Kip about my thoughts – mostly what I had concerns about from a woman's perspective. He playfully teased me with the nickname of "Radar" because in his mind I could "pick up" the minutest details of his conversations so far away!

Soon afterward, Kip trusted me along with the wives of the other Evangelists and Shepherds to be a part of the Staff and Planning Meetings for the purpose of giving our thoughts on: women's issues, the needs of the sisters, the needs of the children, and the financial needs of the churches. This so helped my heart especially on decisions that I would have initially disagreed. Now, since I know the heart behind the decisions, I can by word and by example call all the sisters to "get behind" the decisions that the brothers made for the church. In time, Kip like Jesus, would give women "equal opportunity" to "sit at his feet" to learn the Scriptures at the International College of Christian Ministries (ICCM). In fact, the ICCM has an equal number of women students as men students!

As we close out this book, all women disciples need to continually *ELEVATE* our relationships with God – to get closer to Him. We must fully invest all of our gifts for the honor of God. (Matthew 25:14-30) One of my closest sisters that so radiates the light of Christ is Lianne Kernan. Yet when Tim and Lianne first dated, some doubted that she was "ministry material." And when we first began to get to know the Kernans after they came to the 2004 Portland Jubilee, Lianne did have a predisposition to depression. This weakness has almost completely vanished as Lianne has served valiantly with her incredible husband Tim in London, England; Toronto, Canada; Chennai, India; Paris, France; and now Los Angeles! She shines brightly in doing so much in the ministry and also joyfully raises with Tim their two sons – Junior and David. To add to her blessings last year in Canada, she helped Tim to restore her father – Steph Brown – to the Lord! Today, in 2016, the Kernans are the World Sector Leaders of the Western United States and Canada! And as of December 2015, this precious son and daughter in the faith have assumed the role of leading the Mighty City of Angels International Christian Church and the ICCM – Los Angeles!

Another sister who **ELEVATED** her relationship with God after she had fallen was Lynda (Perdigon) Moreno. Lynda had served God fulltime since she was six months old in the Lord. She courageously served on the mission fields of Brazil, Argentina and Chile. She married the daring Raul Moreno and then together they powerfully led the Santiago International Church of Christ. When our former fellowship (ICOC) was crashing in 2003 – largely because they abandoned discipling and the role of "Overseeing Evangelists" – Raul and Lynda still strove to continue to teach and practice discipling in their congregation. That led them to visit Portland in January 2005, where they asked Kip and me to disciple them in Santiago from Portland.

With this decision for us to disciple them, the Santiago Church began to once again surge in baptizing disciples. However, when the "new movement" officially formed in the fall of 2006, strong criticism arose from the ICOC against the Morenos staying with us and the Portland Movement – now called the SoldOut Movement. So at this juncture, the Morenos "stepped back" mainly because Raul thought that he could change what remained of the ICOC. But in the summer of 2007, when Raul realized that the ICOC was not going to return to the Biblical command of discipling and give up the church governance of autonomy, he made the valiant decision to "rejoin" God's new movement. Sadly, only 15 of the 275 members of the Santiago Church ultimately followed Raul's lead.

When Raul's Biblical stand formed the Santiago Remnant Group in 2007, the Morenos were sinfully "disfellowshipped." Lynda was so distraught over the loss of relationships that she suffered a nervous breakdown. We finally were able to secure enough finances to bring the Morenos to Los Angeles for healing and training in the summer of 2008.

After three years in the City of Angels International Christian Church in Los Angeles, Lynda's soul had been healed and she regained her Biblical convictions that standing up for God's truth will bring division. (Luke 12:51) Lynda's passion for Sao Paulo, Brazil – the first city where she served the Lord fulltime – guided her husband to ask Kip if they could plant the new movement's church in that great city. Today, Raul and Lynda lead one of our fastest growing churches in the SoldOut Movement – the Sao Paulo International Christian Church! Of note, the group that stayed with what is left of the ICOC in Santiago has continued to shrink to under 80 on Sundays. Whereas, the 15 disciples, who shared Raul and Lynda's Biblical convictions of discipling, have multiplied into a church of 200! Now the Santiago International Christian Church is dynamically led by Alfredo and Alejandra Anuch, Chilean nationals who were converted in the campus ministry when Raul and Lynda were leading the Santiago ICOC!

Lynda's awesome husband was a vital key to nursing Lynda back to spiritual health through great patience, gentle words and great weekly Bible studies for their "d-times" (weekly discipling times). During her three years serving the Orange County Region of the City of Angels Church, Lynda's ministry to the campuses bore much fruit that yielded so many future leaders: Margie (Flores) Hamula, Ashley (Watson) Sarkodie, Joaly Carr, Anayeli Castelan, Jennifer Habib, Nathalie (Moningka) Fetelika, and Lynda personally met Mason Fetelika (now Nat's husband) who came to her "All Women's Bible Talk" as his first exposure to the Kingdom! Lynda has continued this abundant fruitfulness on the number one ranked campus in all of Latin America – the University of Sao Paulo! There are presently 50 disciples at this prestigious campus… and growing! Now so dear to us, Raul and Lynda serve as the World Sector Leaders for all of Central and South

America! So no matter how far you have fallen, God can help you rise again and even go beyond your former glory days!

So to *ELEVATE* is to consecrate our hearts, souls, minds and bodies to love and honor God, to participate in God's purposes in His timing, and then to celebrate being God's daughters every day into eternity! So sisters, if you are struggling or even spiritually dead, just as Jesus said to Jairus' beloved daughter, ***"get up"*** – *ELEVATE* – knowing that ***"[God] is able to do immeasurably more than all we ask or imagine, according to His power that is at work within us, to Him be glory in the church and in Christ Jesus throughout [THIS and] all generations, for ever and ever! Amen!"*** (Ephesians 3:20-21)

1.   Ed Vasicek, "Synagogue System And Early Christianity," http://www.highlandpc.com/studies/fojc/synagsys.php

Epilogue

The Gospel of Luke is unique from the other three Gospels with its many references to women. By overviewing all of the other various references to individual women and female associations in the Book of Luke outside of the "Women's Elevation Section," we can truly appreciate Jesus' extraordinary vision for all women in all nations!

Elizabeth – (Luke 1:5-25; 39-45; 56-66) The wife of Zechariah, mother of John the Baptist, and cousin of Mary – the mother of Jesus. In sharp contrast to Zechariah who served as a priest, Elizabeth immediately believed the seemingly "impossible prophecy" that she would bear a child in her old age. (Luke 1:37 NIV 1984)

Mary of Nazareth – (Luke 1:26-56; 2:4-52; 8:19-21; 11:27-28; 23:49; 24:10) The mother of Jesus and wife of Joseph. Most likely Mary was around 14 years old when the angel Gabriel announces to her that she was favored above all women. Mary miraculously becomes pregnant as a virgin through the Holy Spirit and gives birth to **"the Son of God."** Her trusting, obedient response to Gabriel's reminder that **"nothing is impossible with God"** is an upward call to all women and men of all time, **"I am the Lord's servant... may it be to me as you have said."** In the "original Gospel" of Mark, the question comes about Jesus, **"Isn't this Mary's son and the brother of James, Joseph, Judas and Simon?"** (Mark 6:3) Since Luke "borrows" from the Gospel of Mark, we can be certain that the reference in Luke 24:10 **"the mother of James"** is indeed Mary, the mother of Jesus, who with the other women told the Apostles the news of Jesus' resurrection! (Mark 16:1) In addition, Jesus speaks some of His last words before His death to His beloved mother Mary when He told her that the Apostle John would take care of her as a son. (John 19:25-27)

Interestingly, since the Gospel of Luke is constructed from eyewitness accounts, Mary must have been one of these eyewitnesses. (Luke 1:2) Such details as **"Mary treasured up all these things and pondered them in her heart"** points to this conclusion. (Luke 2:19) This sense of intricate knowledge that could only be gleaned from a direct conversation with Mary is again highlighted in Luke 2:51 after the account of Jesus at the Temple when He was 12 years old, **"[Jesus'] mother treasured all these things in her heart."** Luke, like Jesus and Luke's discipler Paul, respected women's perspectives, believed their words, and held their testimony in equal regard to the accounts of men.

Anna – (Luke 2:36-38) The 84 year old prophetess who spoke about the baby Jesus as **"the redemption of Jerusalem."**

Herodias – (Luke 3:19-20) The unlawful wife of Herod the Tetrarch who previously was married to Herod's brother Philip. Herodias' grudge against John the Baptist for confronting this sin, led to John's beheading. This martyrdom was instigated by Herodias' daughter – known in history as Salome. Salome's seductive dance before Herod at his birthday banquet so captivated him and all his guests that Herod said that he would grant to Salome any request up to half the kingdom. Salome asked her mother what to request. Herodias quickly replies,

"The head of John the Baptist." (Mark 6:17-28) Later this most likely erotic dance became iconized as the "Dance of the Seven Veils."

Widow of Zarephath – (Luke 4:26) Jesus used this reference to this Gentile widow saved from famine by Elijah to show that God has always wanted to "preach good news" to the Gentiles, as well as to the Jews.

Simon's Mother-in-law – (Luke 4:38-39) Peter's mother-in-law is healed by Jesus as the first thing He did upon entering the home of Peter after leaving the synagogue in Capernaum. This indicates that Peter was married, which is contrary to the popular belief that Peter was celibate.

Bridegroom's Bride – (Luke 5:34-35) Though the bride of Jesus is only alluded to in this passage, we understand that the bride of Christ is the church. (Ephesians 5:22-32; Revelation 21:2-3)

Martha of Bethany – (Luke 10:38-42) The most likely older sister of Mary of Bethany and Lazarus. (John 11:1-2) She was loved by Jesus, yet wrestled with being consumed with worry. (Luke 10:41-42)

Mary of Bethany – (Luke 7:36-50; 10:38-42) Most likely the younger sister of Martha and Lazarus, as Martha owned their home. (Luke 10:38; John 11:1-2) She is the woman who anointed Jesus as recorded in not only Luke 7, but also in Matthew 26:6-13, Mark 14:3-9, and John12:1-8. Matthew also places her with Mary Magdalene attending Jesus' tomb. (Matthew 28:1)

Queen of the South – (Luke 11:31) This is the Queen of Sheba, who visits Solomon. (1 Kings 10:1-13; 2 Chronicles 9:1-12)

Divided female family relationships – (Luke 12:51-53) When the good news is preached division will come: *"Mother against daughter and daughter against mother, mother-in-law against daughter-in-law and daughter-in-law against mother-in-law."* Much later Jesus warned His disciples in Luke 21:16 that they *"will be betrayed even by parents, brothers, sisters, relatives and friends, and they will put some of you to death."* Our commitment to Christ must supersede our love for our precious family members without compromise even to the point of death.

Crippled Woman – (Luke 13:10-17) This woman was bent over and unable to straighten up for 18 long years. Jesus heals her in the synagogue on the Sabbath purposely exposing the hypocrisy ("the bending" or twisting of the Scriptures) of His religious opponents.

Baker Woman – (Luke 13:20-21) This parable of the woman who puts in yeast that works through the whole dough is in "balance" of the previous short parable of the man who plants a mustard seed that grows into a large tree where (inferred – all) birds of the air perched in its branches. Both parables speak about world evangelism: the whole dough and "all birds" represent all nations. Also, the literary device of "balance" is used collectively by the two parables: the first about a man and the other about a woman. Therefore, man + woman = the whole world.

Hen – (Luke 13:34-35) Jesus uses a beautiful and touching female illustration about a hen gathering her chicks which parallels His love for Jerusalem. God (Jesus) has all male and female attributes, as *"God created mankind in His own image... male and female He created them."* (Genesis 1:27)

Newlywed Woman – (Luke 14:20) The newlywed man – who loves his new wife – believes this highlight in his life of marriage is a higher priority above coming to the Great Kingdom Banquet. Jesus implies that – weddings and spouses – cannot be an excuse at any time to not be a disciple. This is again reiterated in Luke 14:26, *"If anyone comes to me and does not hate father and mother, wife and children, brothers and sisters – yes, even their own life – such a person cannot be my disciple."* Later in Luke 18:29-30, Jesus re-engages this point, *"Truly I tell you… no one who has left home or wife or brothers or sisters or parents or children for the sake of the Kingdom of God will fail to receive many time as much in this age and, I the age to come eternal life."*

The Woman with 10 silver coins – (Luke 15:8-10) This woman loses one silver coin. The coin is an inanimate object which cannot find its way back to its owner, so the woman must search with a lit lamp as her guide in order for the coin to be found. The woman is the church which is guided by the light (Holy Spirit) in *"seeking and saving"* lost souls which by themselves cannot be saved. (Luke 19:10) Upon finding the coin, the woman and her friends rejoice as *"there is rejoicing in the presence of the angels of God over one sinner who repents."*

Prostitutes – (Luke 15:30) In the Parable of the Lost Sons, the younger son *"squandered his wealth in wild living"* which included going to prostitutes. The older son is also lost, as he is outside his father's house and refuses to go in. (Luke 15:28) The sins that keep the older son from God are not as "in your face" as going to prostitutes. However, the sins of jealousy, entitlement, bitterness and anger have separated him from his father – who represents God. Amazingly, those who go to prostitutes and the prostitutes themselves can be forgiven through repentance and grace granting them a personal relationship with God. (Luke 15:32; 1 Corinthians 6:6-9) In fact, Jesus said to the chief priest and elders of the people, *"I tell you the truth, the tax collectors and the prostitutes are entering the Kingdom of God ahead of you."* (Matthew 21:23, 31)

Lot's Wife – (Luke 17:30-36) Though Lot's wife was being led away by angels from the destruction of Sodom to safety, she was enticed by the world and *"looked back."* (Genesis 19:26) Lot's wife was immediately turned into a pillar of salt. Indeed, there will be difficult moments in our Christian journey, but we can never look back rationalizing that our former life in the world was "easier" therefore "better" than our walk with Christ. However, if one succumbs to this temptation to live a compromised Christian life by trying **"to keep [one's] life, [one] will lose it."** So, the ultimate reason not to compromise one's convictions is summed up in Luke 17:35 in the judgment of the two women in the same circumstance (grinding) – one is saved and the other is lost. Circumstances do not and must not determine our salvation; it is one's individual decision despite the circumstances *"to follow Jesus, no turning back!"*

Persistent Widow – (Luke 18:1-8) This woman – who has no husband to help her – teaches us to **"always pray and not give up."** Jesus uses the example of a woman in this parable as an upward call to His disciples – both male and female.

People bringing babies to Jesus – (Luke 18:15-17) Seemingly both dads and moms were bringing their baby boys and baby girls to Jesus for Him to bless them. As well, the children that were old enough to walk were called by Jesus to come to Him. Jesus then challenged His followers to have the hearts of children: trusting, innocent and pure. Jesus also says not to **"hinder"** the little children. We must have a heart to take care of children. It is so sad when disciples turn down opportunities to serve in "Kids Kingdom" (Sunday School), because they "prefer" being in the adult worship service more. These disciples are "missing out" on the joy that a grateful child can bring to his teacher, as well as falling short of the heart of Jesus in His affection for children.

Mothers of Honor – (Luke 18:20) The Bible calls us to honor our fathers and mothers. (Ephesians 6:1-2) Also, Jesus taught us to honor our "spiritual mothers." (Mark 3:33-35) The Apostle Paul honored his "spiritual mom." (Romans 16:13)

Seven-time Married Woman – (Luke 20:27-39) This hypothetical situation proposed by the Sadducees – who did not believe in the resurrection – allowed Jesus to not only teach that there is a resurrection, but that there is no marriage in Heaven. Therefore, one of the primary purposes of marriage is to get our spouse to Heaven.

Sacrificing Widow – (Luke 21:1-4) We learn that Jesus watches our giving and lifts up this woman as an example to all disciples as one who totally trusts God in her giving. Interestingly, in the previous paragraph in Luke 20:45-47, Jesus told the people to *"beware of the teachers of the Law… [who] devour widows' houses…"* In other words, these unscrupulous men were taking advantage of the helpless widows by taking their homes likely through getting them to "legally" give their homes as "inheritances" to the teachers of the law. The widows were persuaded that in this way, they were giving their inheritances to God. These evil teachers of the Law used this "extra income" for their good pleasure. Notice that in Luke 21, Jesus did not tell the widow not to give because of how the finances were used. In fact, He commended her giving. Quite interestingly in Luke 22:4-6, money was given from the Temple treasury to Judas to betray Jesus. Even if we question how "church money is spent," we should have the faith and the heart of the sacrificing widow and never hold back from giving to God.

Servant Girl – (Luke 22:56) On the same night that Jesus was betrayed by Judas, Peter was confronted as being a follower of Jesus by one of the servant girls of the high priest. He faltered in this the first of his three denials that fateful night. (Mark 14:66-68; John 18:15-17) How remarkable is the change in this preacher on the Day of Pentecost where 3,000 were baptized, from the man who cowered before a servant girl just 50 days earlier. Believing in the resurrected Christ and having the Holy Spirit radically changed Peter forever.

Church tradition holds that Peter and his wife died in Rome in 67AD. They were arrested and charged with treason. At Peter's trial, the judge said that he would spare his wife, if Peter would renounce Jesus and say, "Caesar is Lord." At this moment, his wife turned to Peter and simply said, "Remember the Lord!" She was then crucified before Peter's eyes. Peter then requested, "I am not fit to be crucified like my Savior and my wife. Crucify me upside down!" And so he was. Indeed, Peter, his wife and all the brothers and sisters in the early church **"turned the world upside down for Jesus!"** (Acts 17:6 RSV)

Daughters of Jerusalem – (Luke 23:27-31) As Jesus was led to Golgotha, He directed the weeping women not to wail for Him but for themselves and their children. In retrospect, we understand that Jesus was referring to God's judgment on Jerusalem through the Romans in 70AD when the Roman army totally ransacked this city and destroyed the Temple. The Roman historian Josephus claimed that 1.1 million people were slaughtered and that the remaining 97,000 were taken into slavery.

Women Followers from Galilee – (Luke 23:49, 55-56; 24:1-12) The women followers from Galilee had **"cared for [Jesus'] needs"** for three years up to this time of the crucifixion. (Mark 15:41) However, even these loyal followers of Jesus **"stood at a distance"** at the cross. (Luke 23:49) Included were: **"Mary Magdalene, Mary the mother of James and Joseph [Jesus' mother], and the mother of Zebedee's sons [Salome]."** (Matthew 27:55-56; Mark 15:40) Later, **"the women who had come with Jesus from Galilee followed Joseph and saw the tomb where Jesus' body was laid... They prepared spices... rested on the Sabbath... and on the first day of the week... the women took the spices they had prepared and went to the tomb."** The two angels (a signal to Jews of truth – a testimony of two witnesses) jubilantly told the women, **"He is not here; He is risen!"** When the women enthusiastically shared this awesome news to the Eleven, **"They did not believe the women, because their words seemed to them like nonsense."** (Luke 24:11) The Apostles still had not *ELEVATED* women to be a believable source. However, Peter and John – **"amazed by the women's news"** –

ran to see the empty tomb and were bewildered. (Luke 24:22-23) Astoundingly, the tremendous honor of the first person to see and touch Jesus after His resurrection went to a woman – Mary Magdalene! (John 20:11-18)

So, the Gospel of Luke and his Book of Acts dramatically emphasize that the "Spiritual Global Revolution" of Jesus was for all nations – for all men and equally for all women! After reading the Scriptures in the Women's Elevation Section of Luke, will you now *ELEVATE* and join Jesus' cause to change the world in this generation?

Bibliography

1. Psikta Rabbati 43:27

2. James, Carolyn Custis. Half the Church. Grand Rapids, Michigan: Zondervan, 2011.

3. James, Carolyn Custis. Lost Women Of The Bible. Grand Rapids, Michigan: Zondervan, 2005.

4. Steinburg, Stephanie. "What To Do If Your Child Is Cutting," US News And World Report, (February 2014) http://health.usnews.com/health-news/health-wellness/articles/2014/02/28/what-to-do-if-your-child-is-cutting

5. Redford, Gabrielle de Groot. "Why Sleep Is Precious," AARP, December 2014.

6. Vasicek, Ed "Synagogue System And Early Christianity," http://www.highlandpc.com/studies/fojc/synagsys.php

Dear Lana May you enjoy this
book, it is a joy knowing you!
I enjoy our talks, and cherish
your advices.

To: Lana Gordon
from: Mayfern Hydes

Love you sis!